Copyright © 2020 Adults Coloring Book
By Majestic Mandala Publishing,
All rights reserved.

Color Test Page

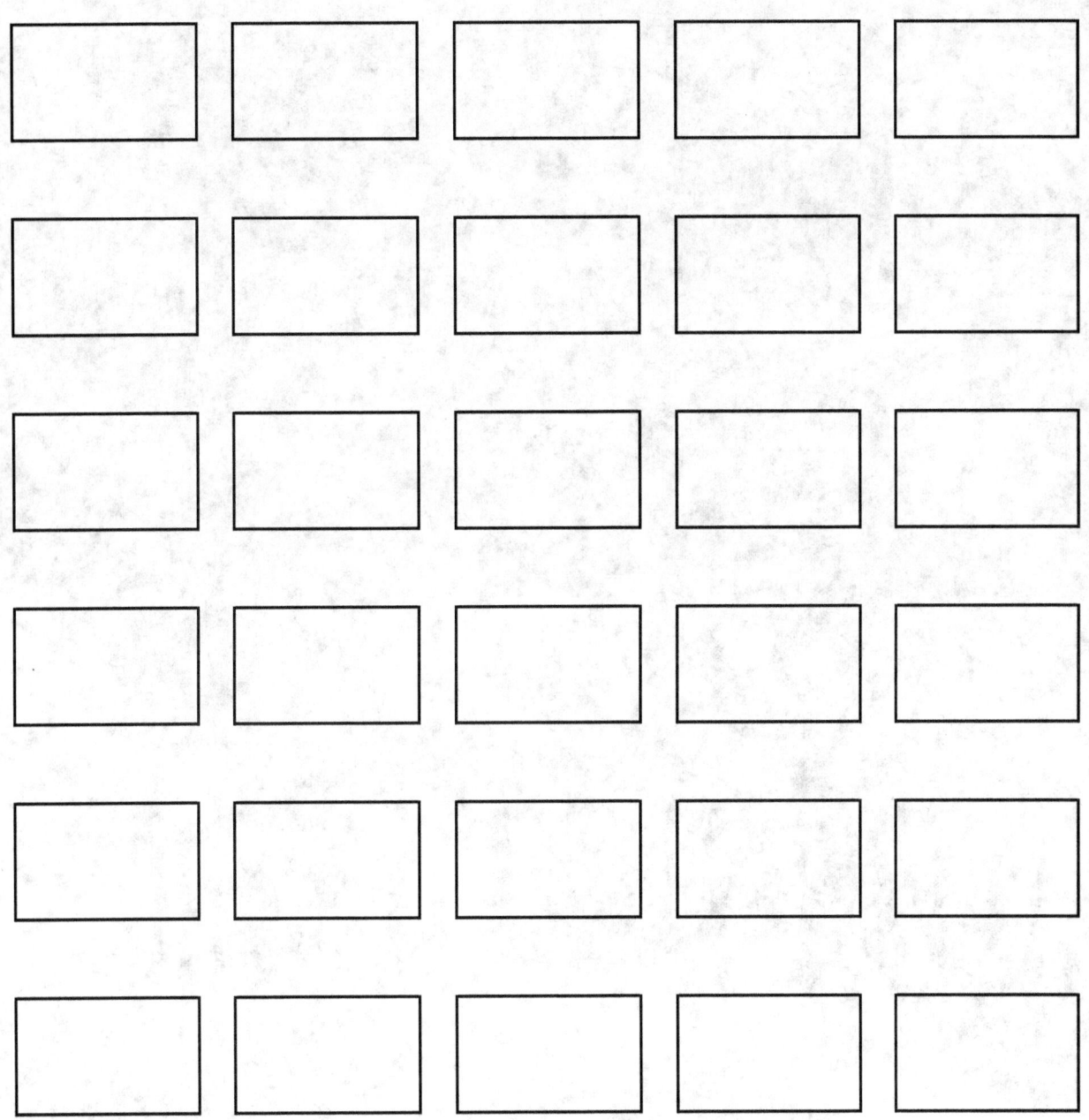

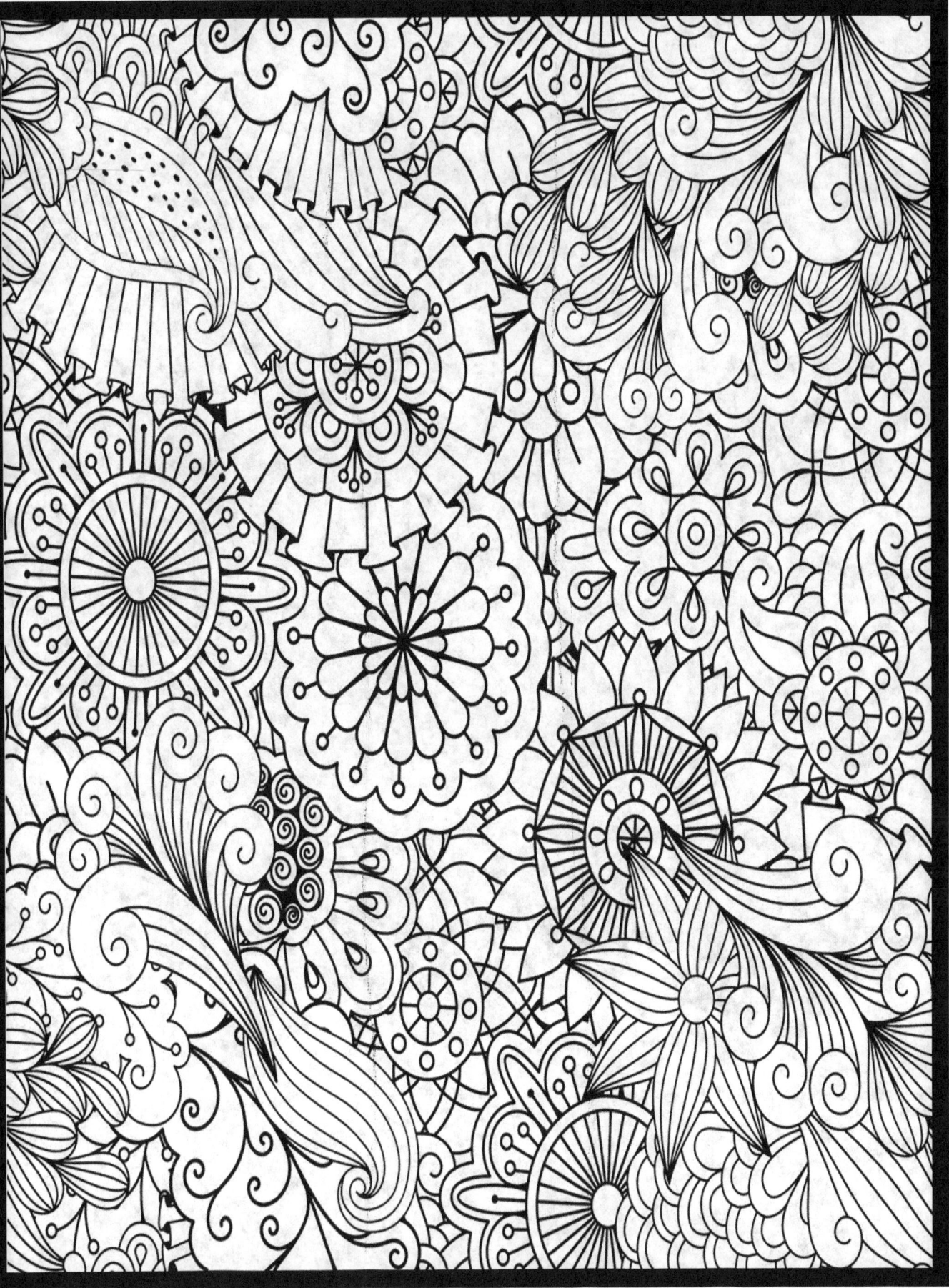

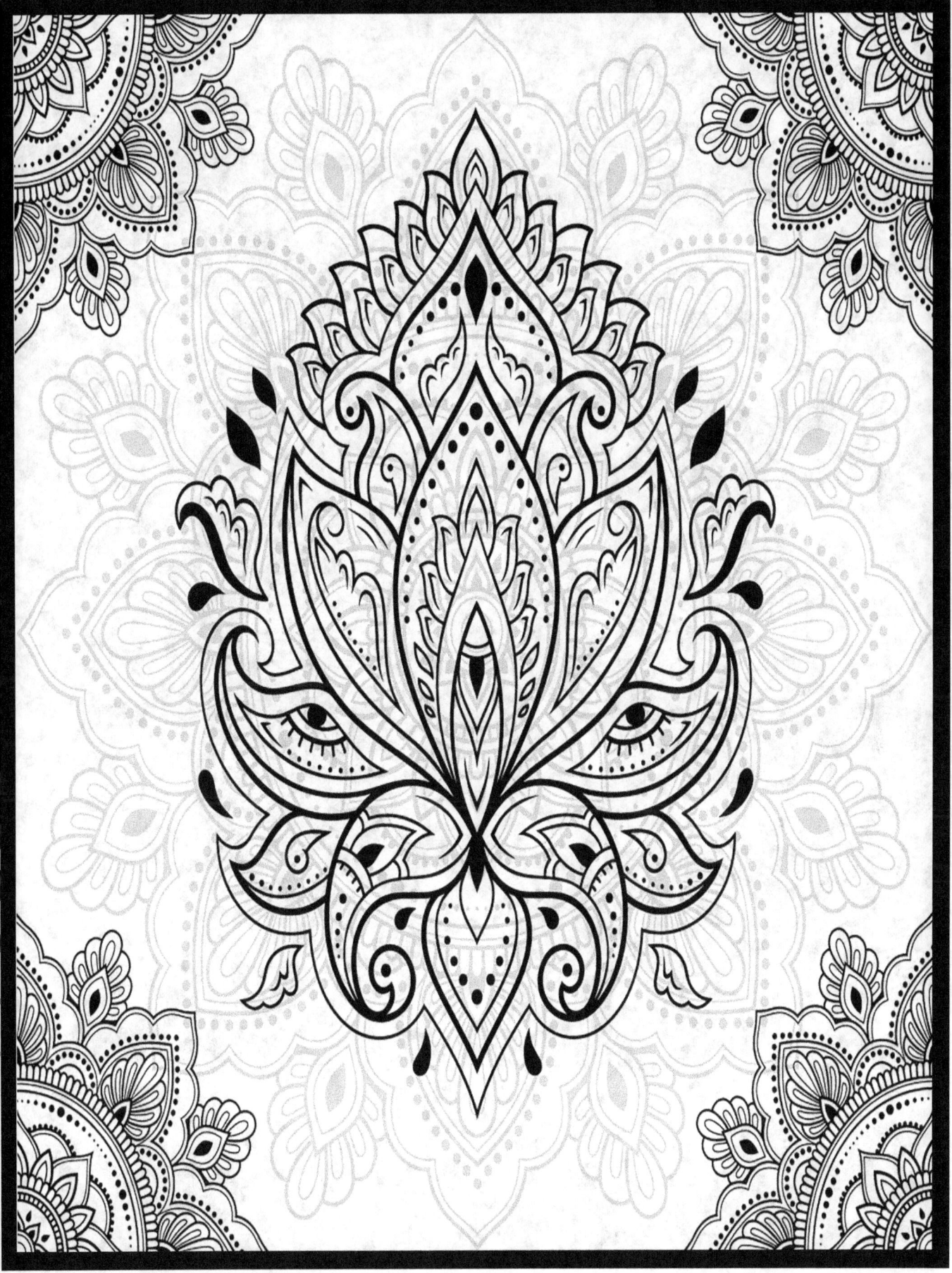

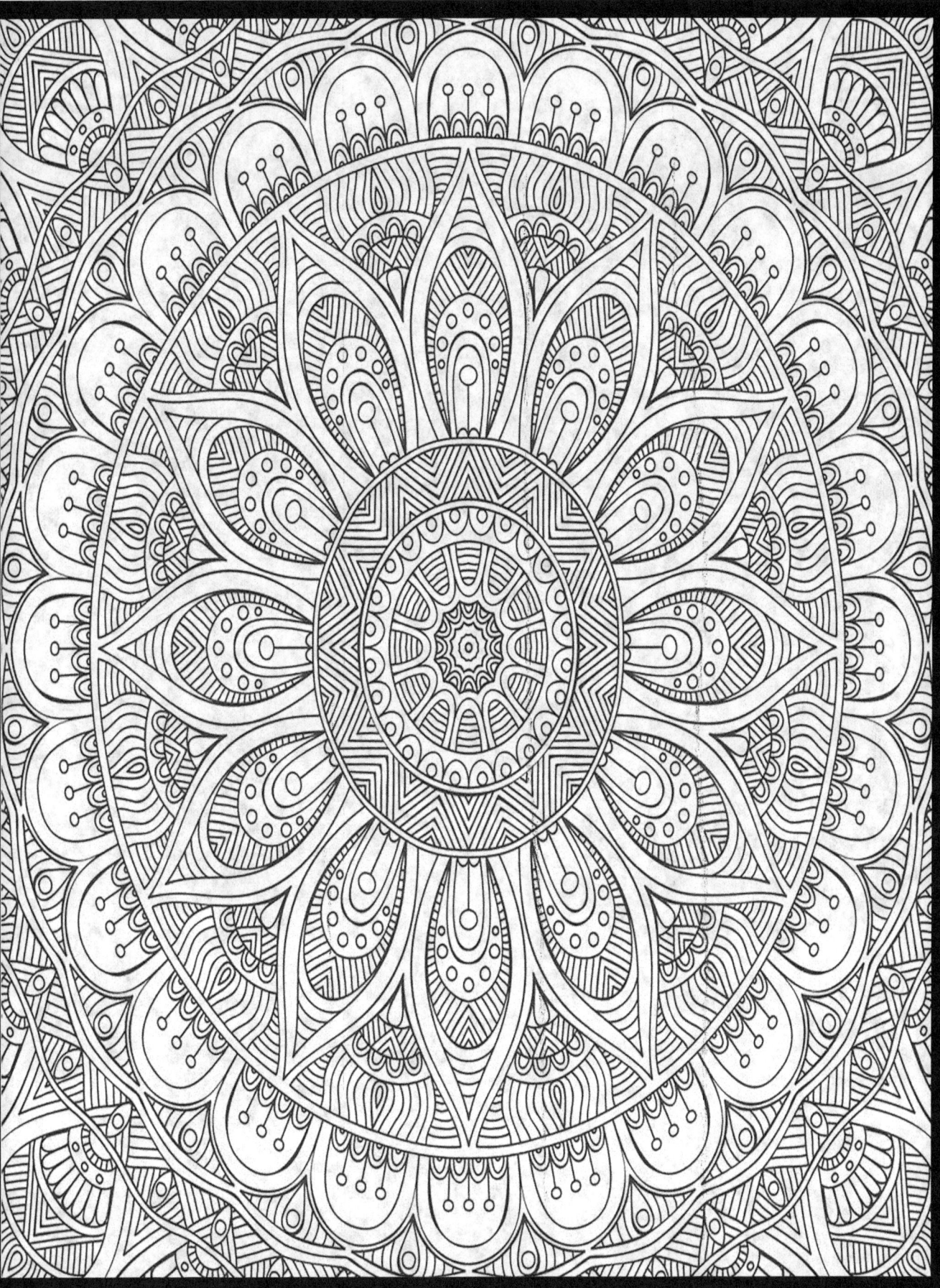

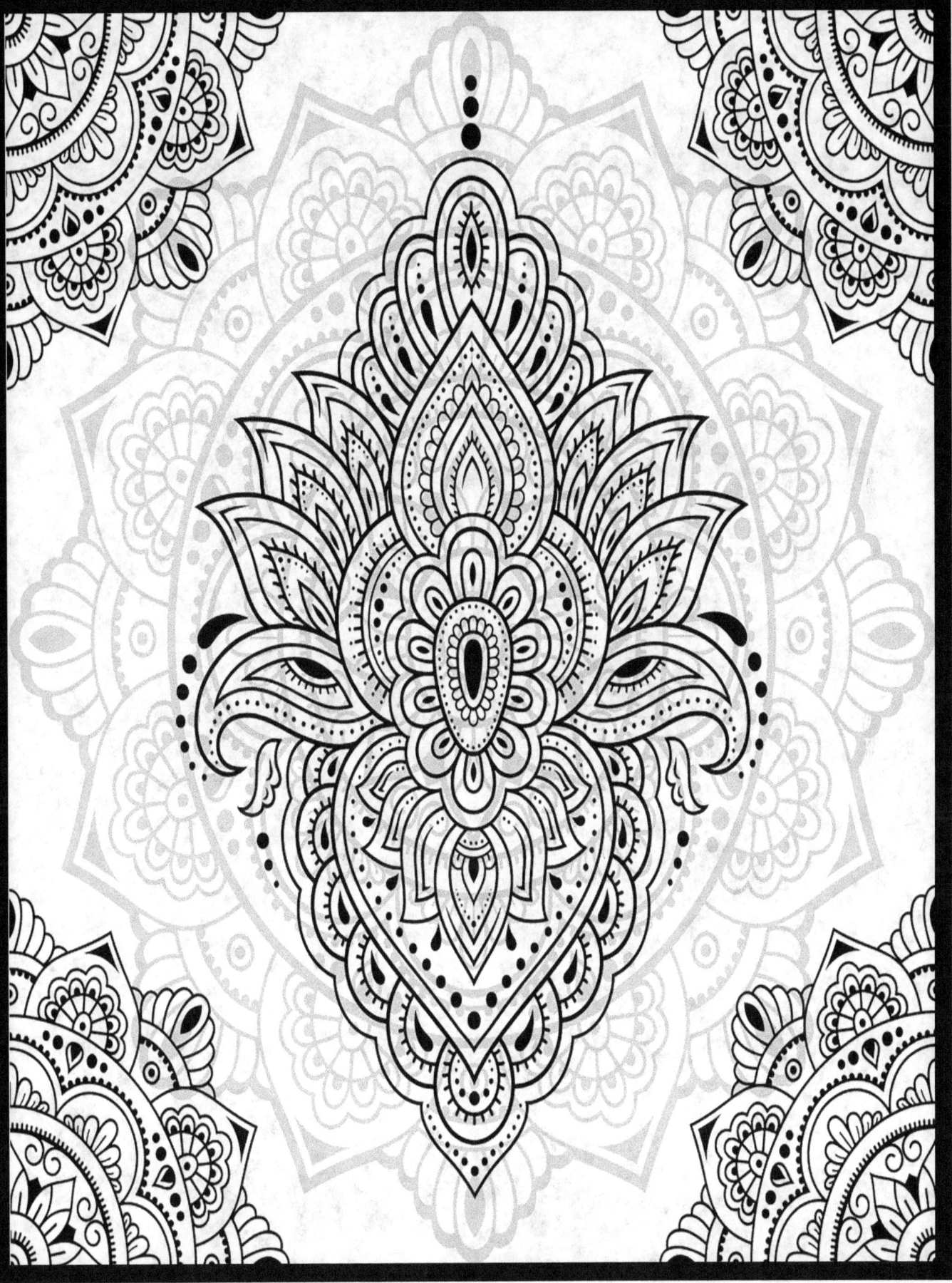

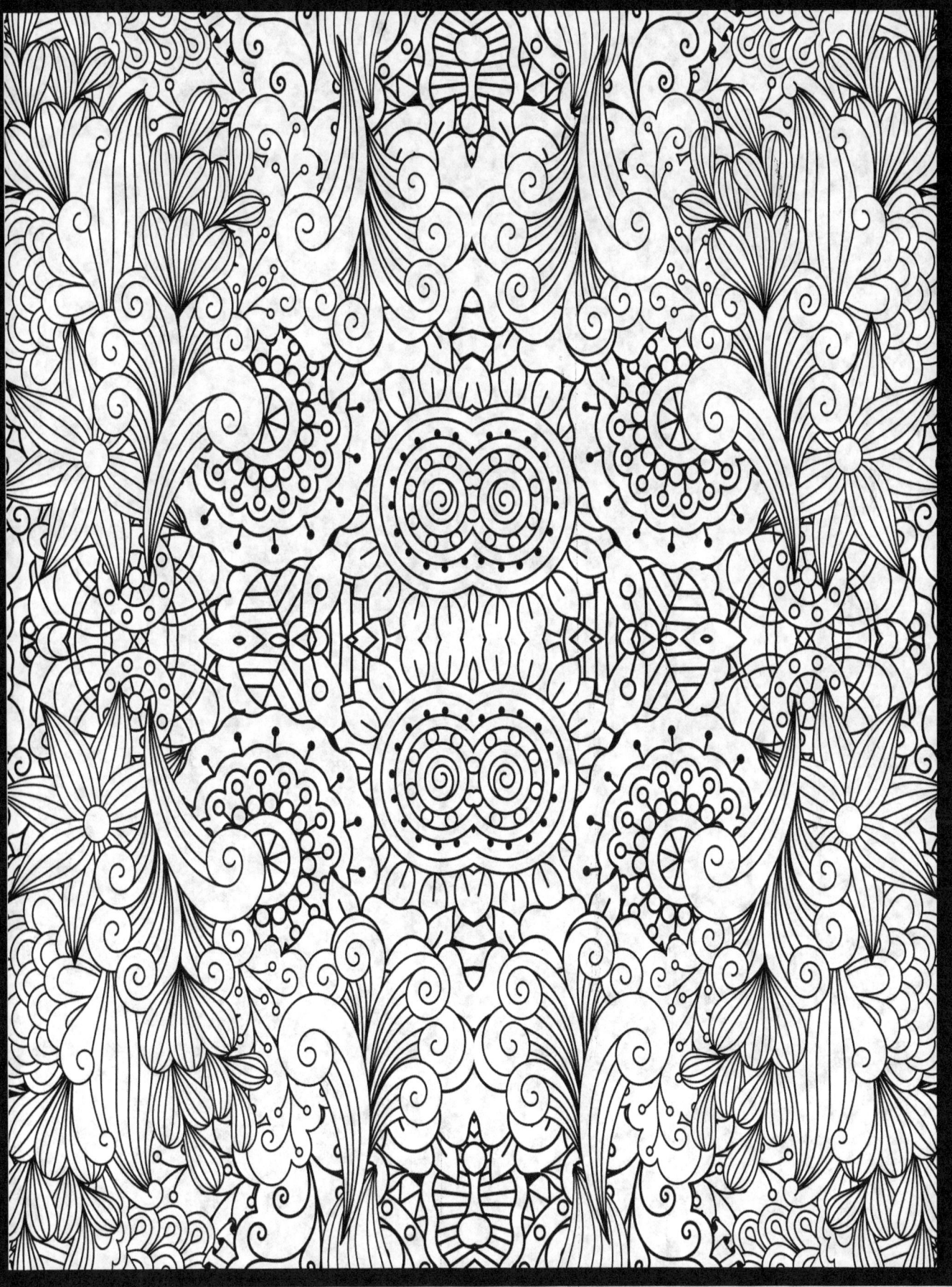

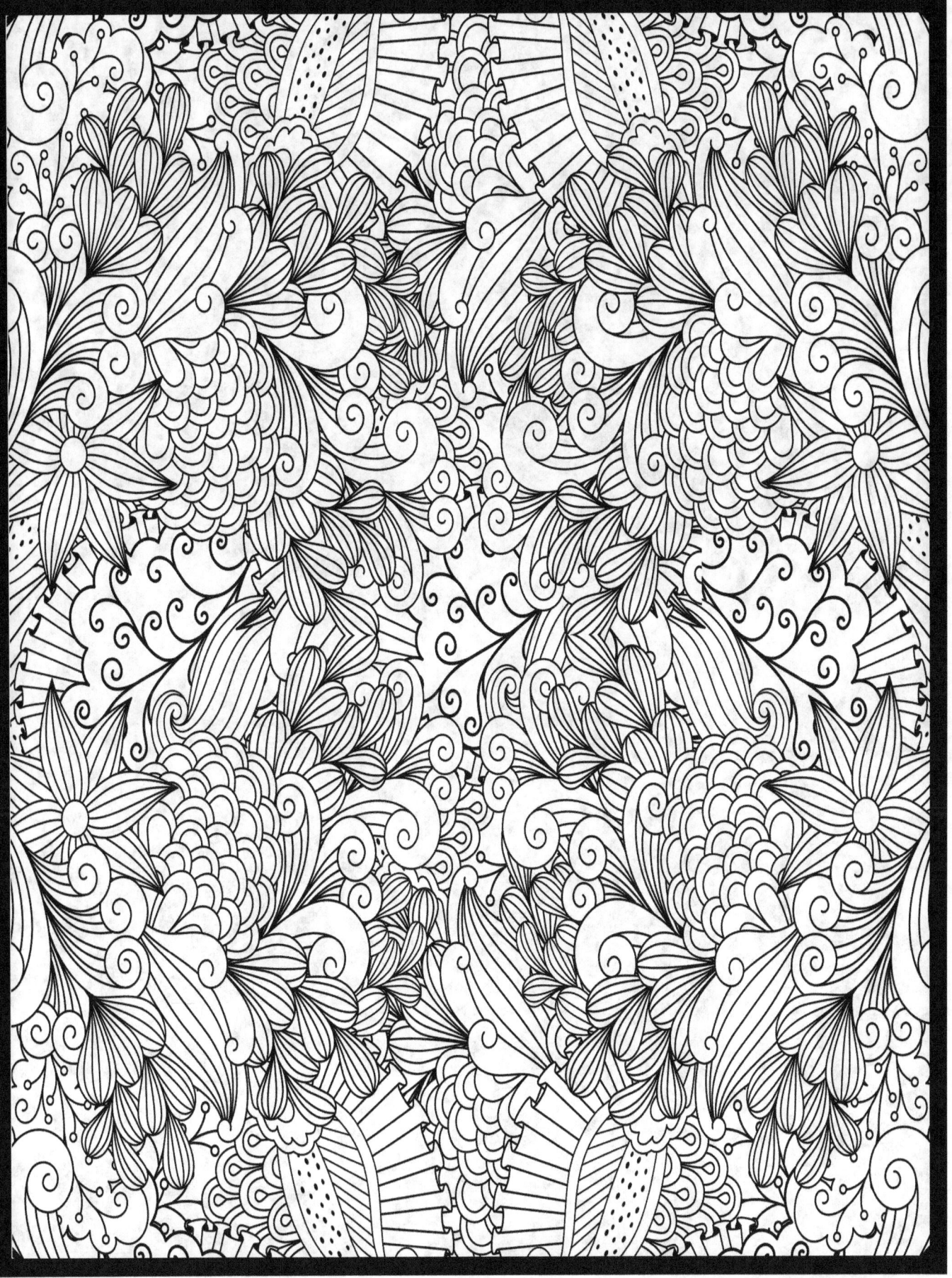

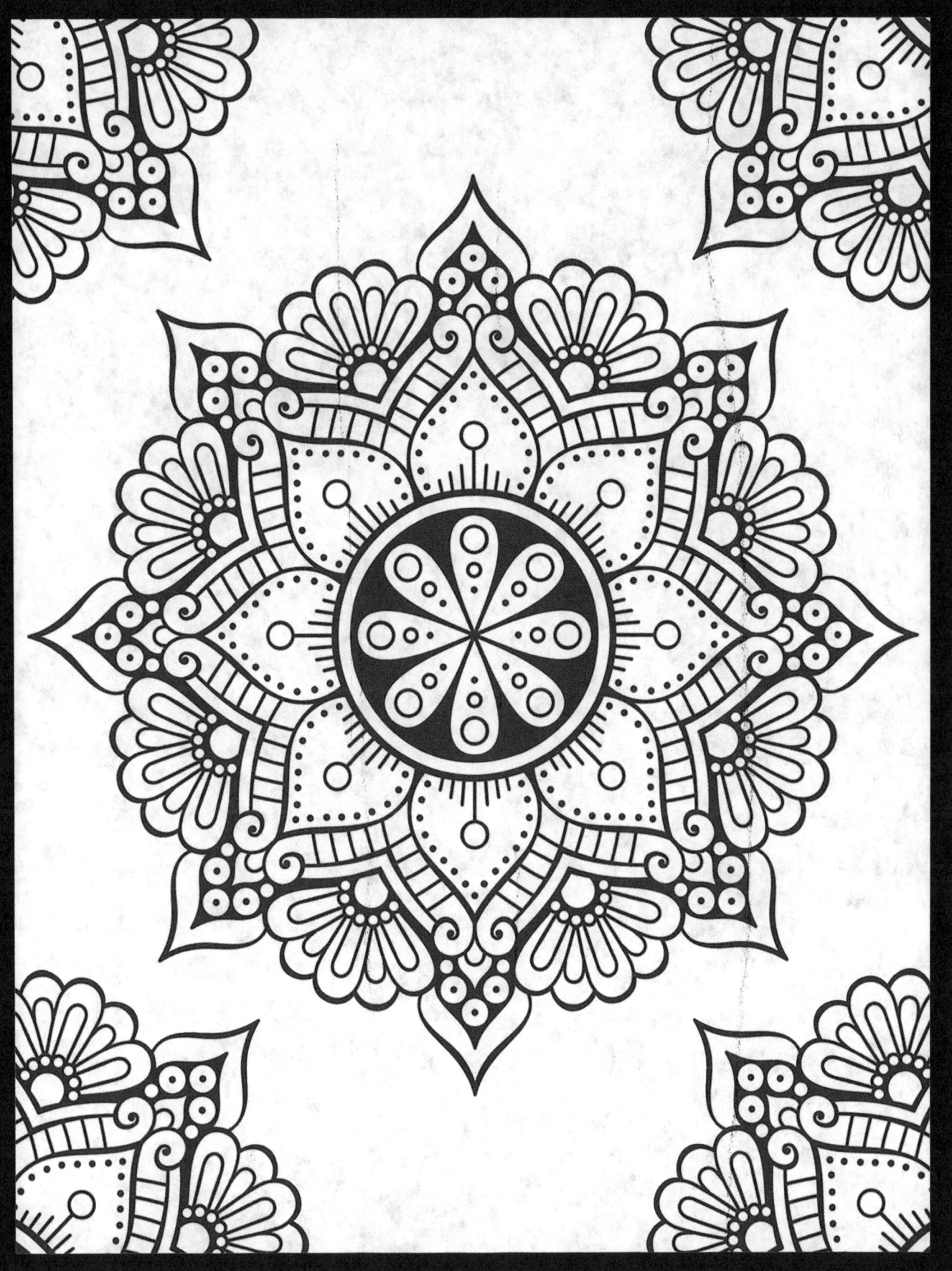

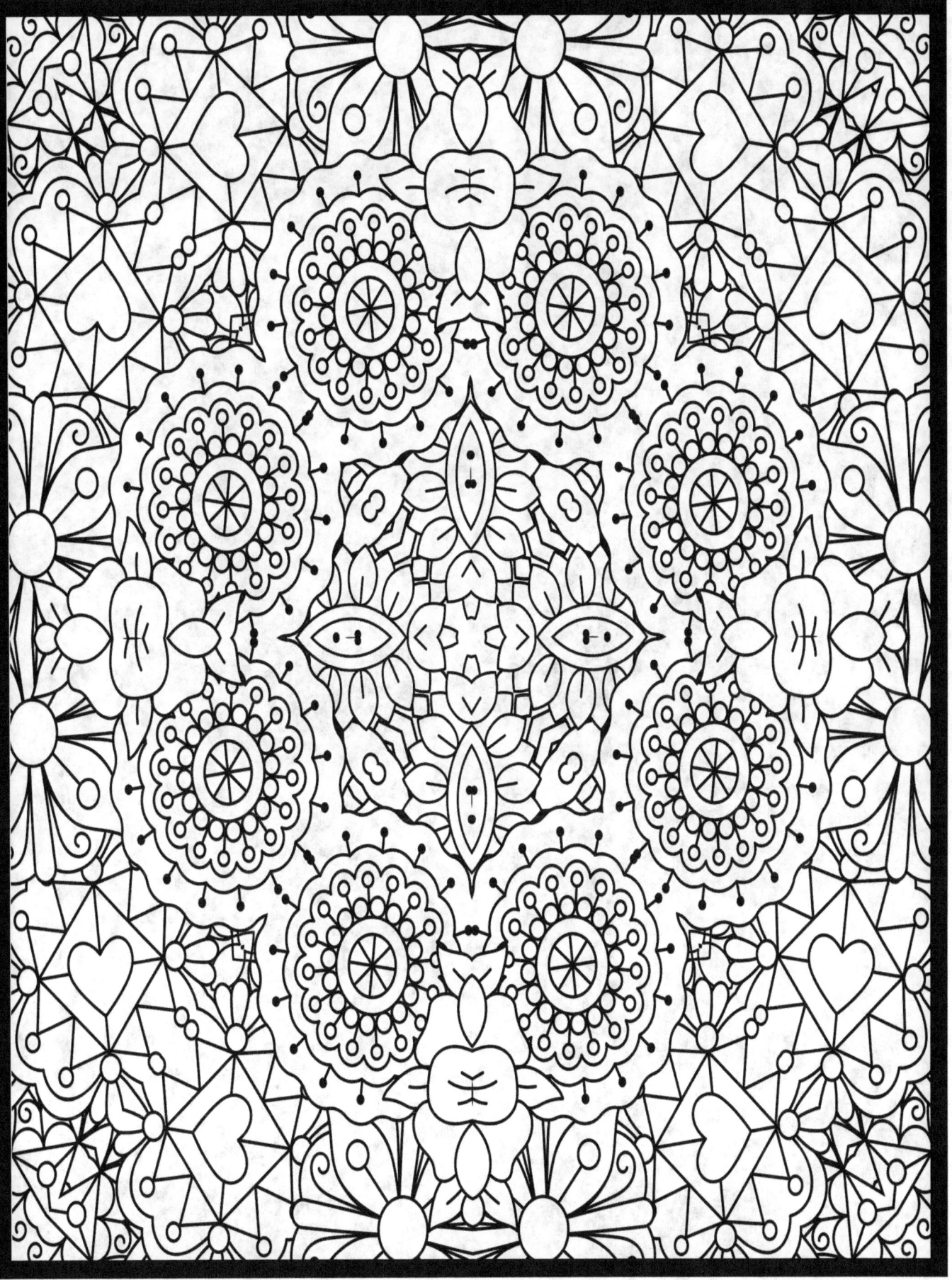

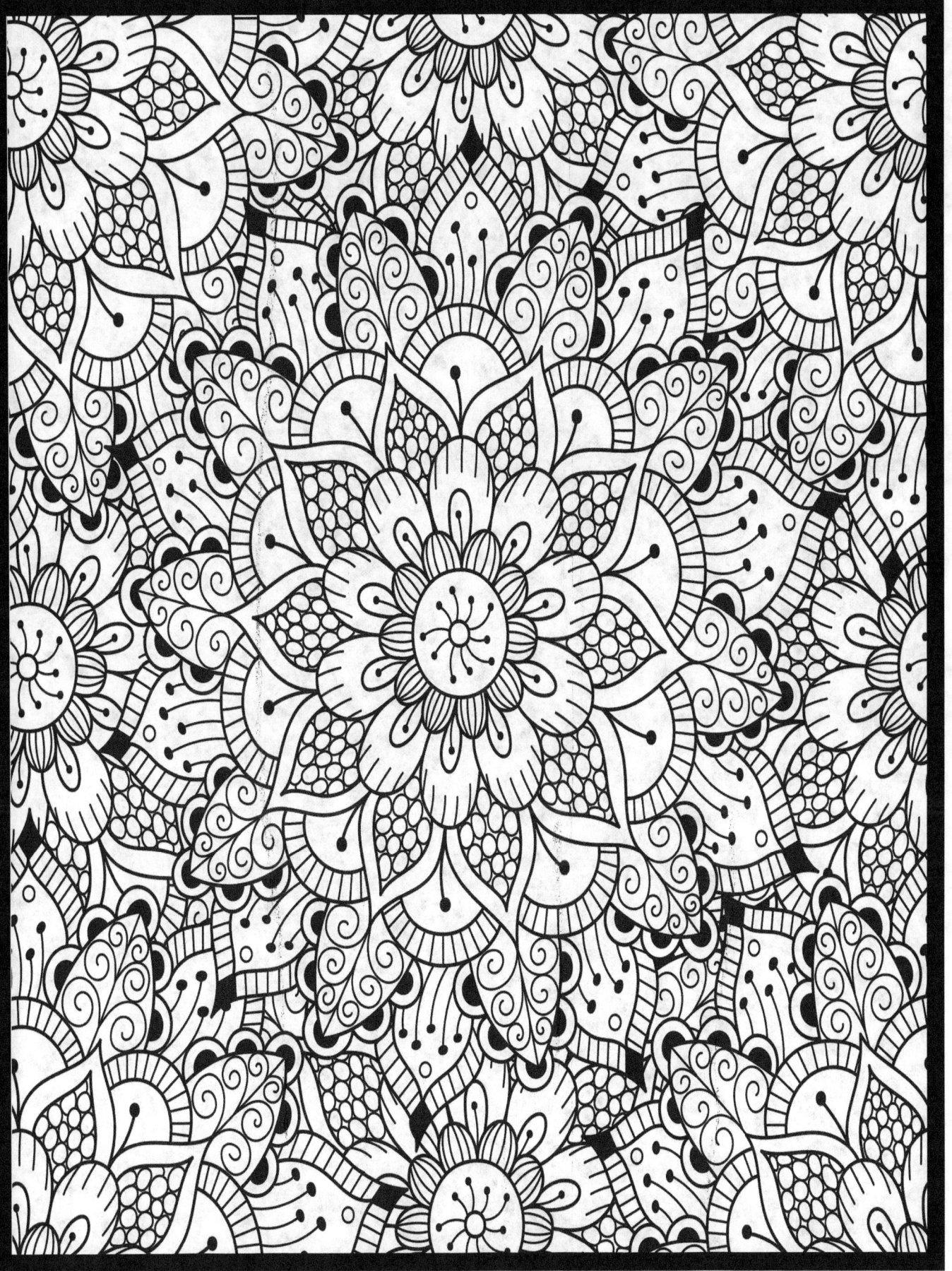

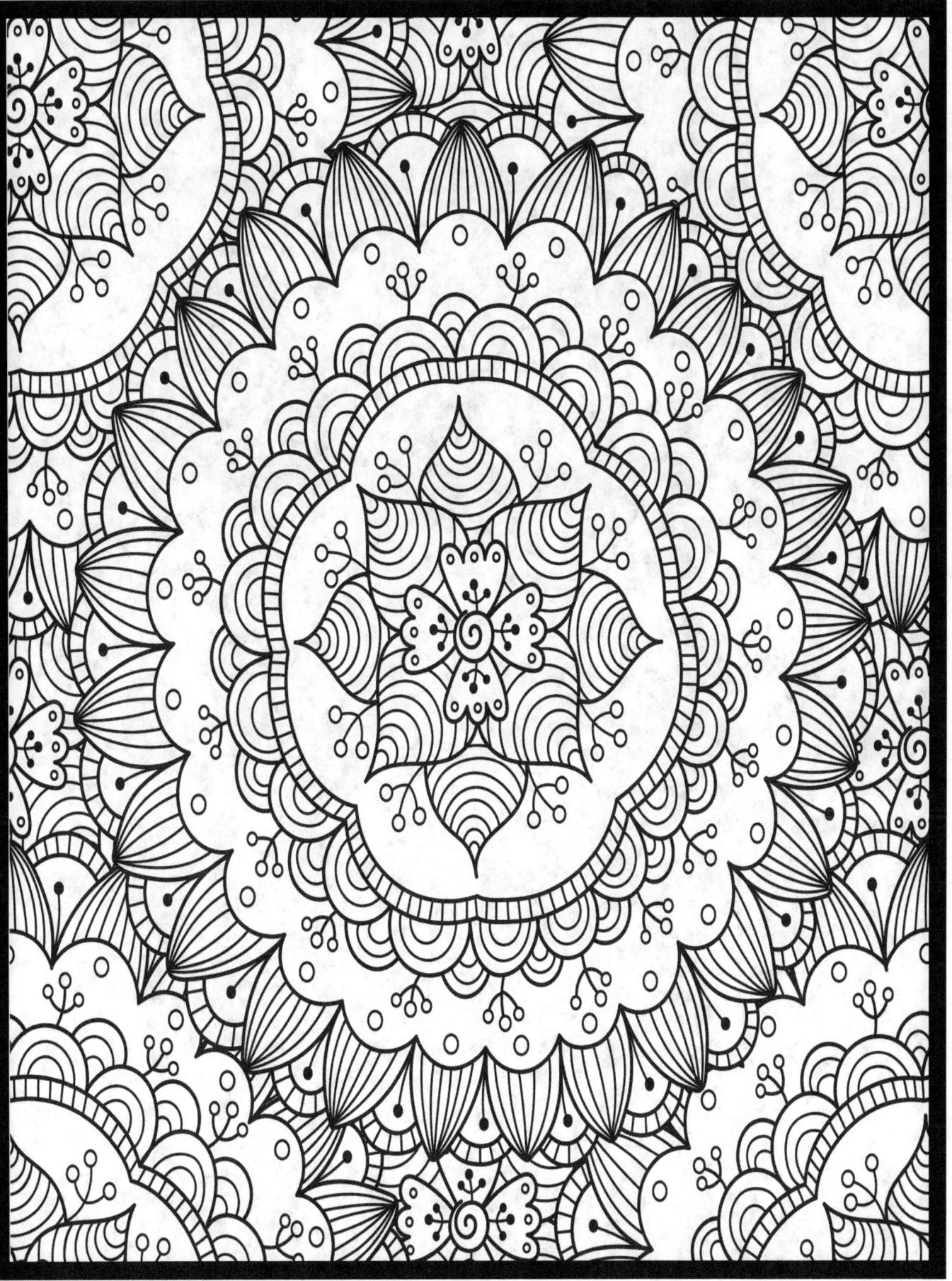

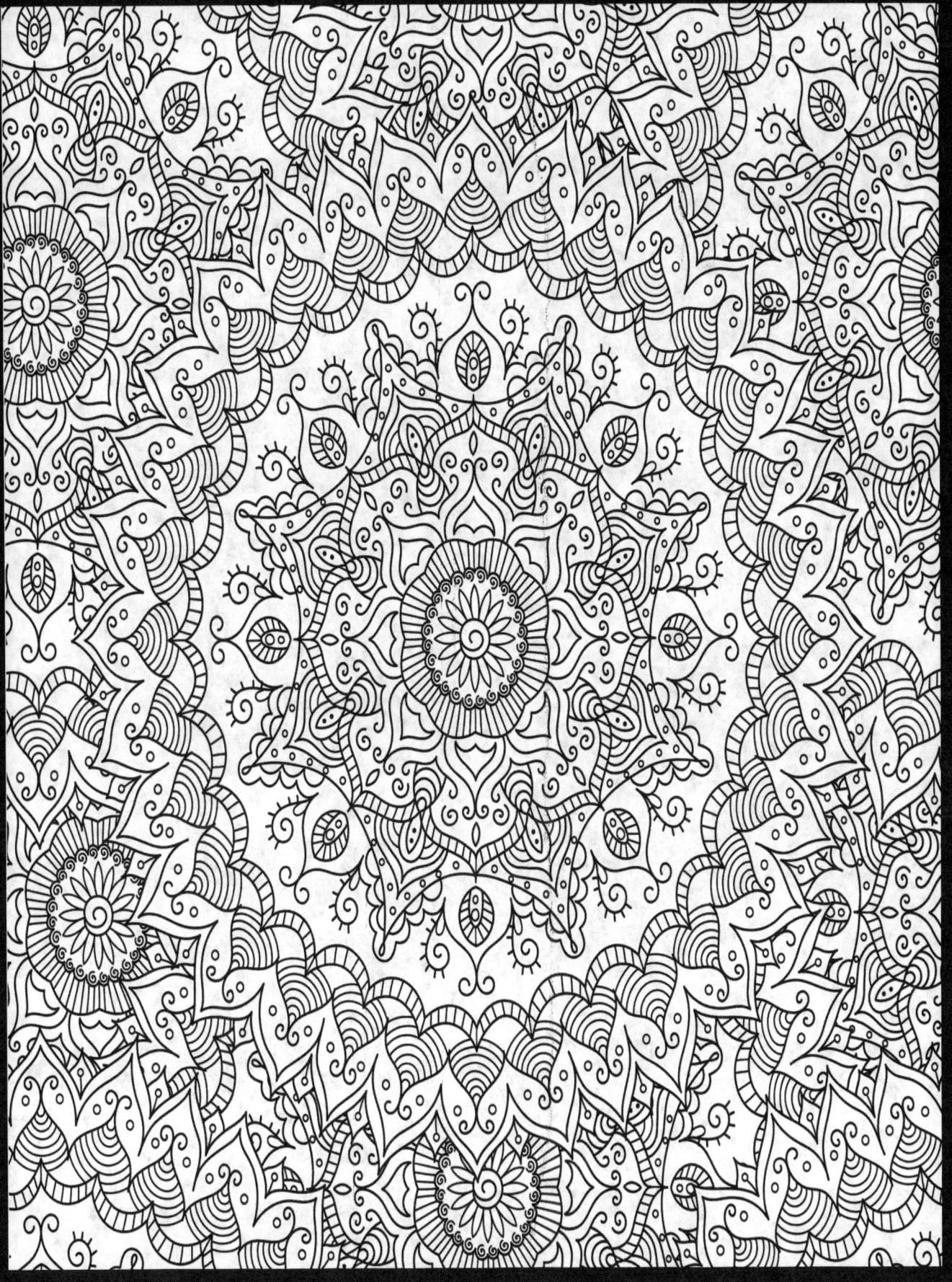

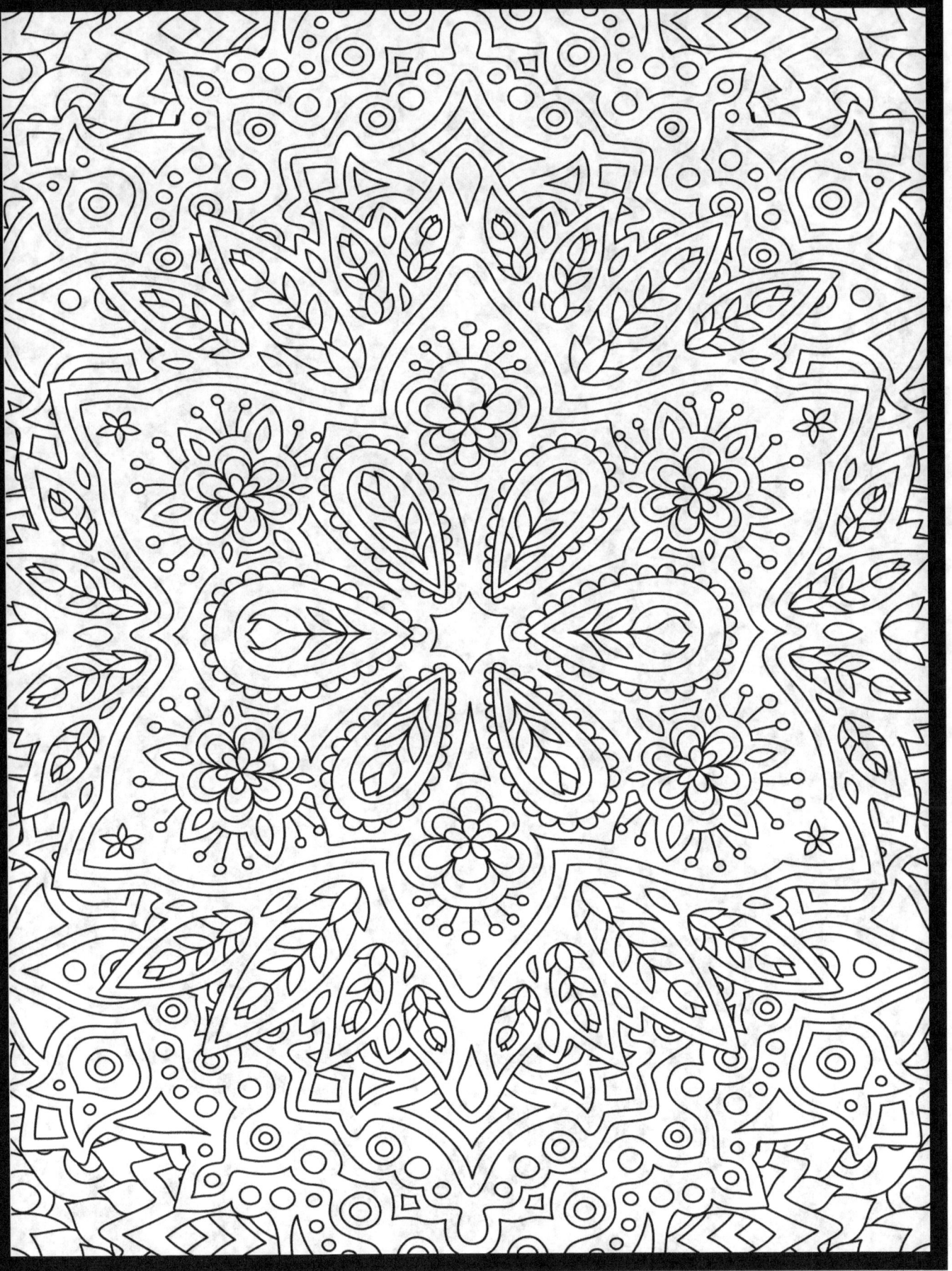

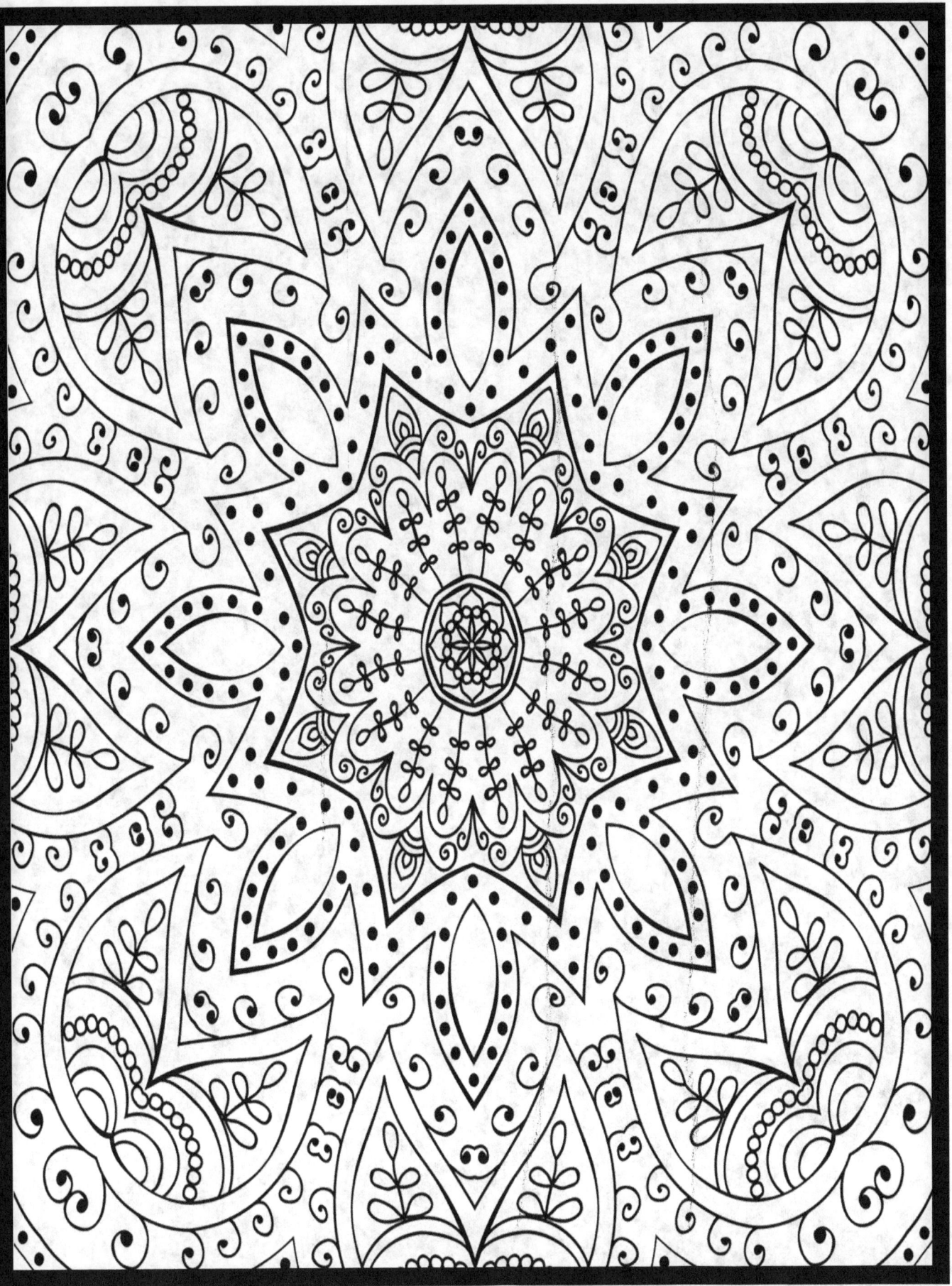

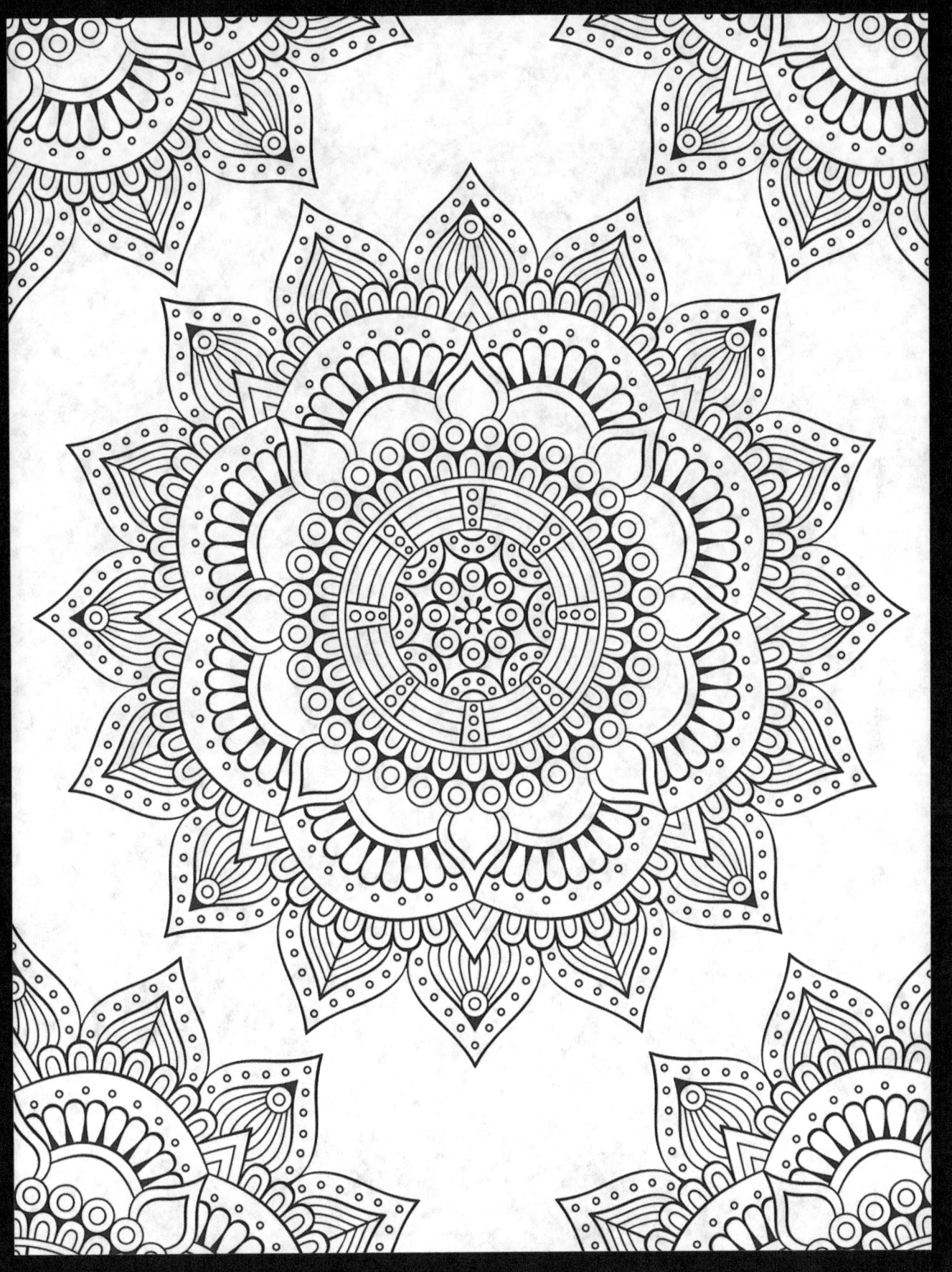

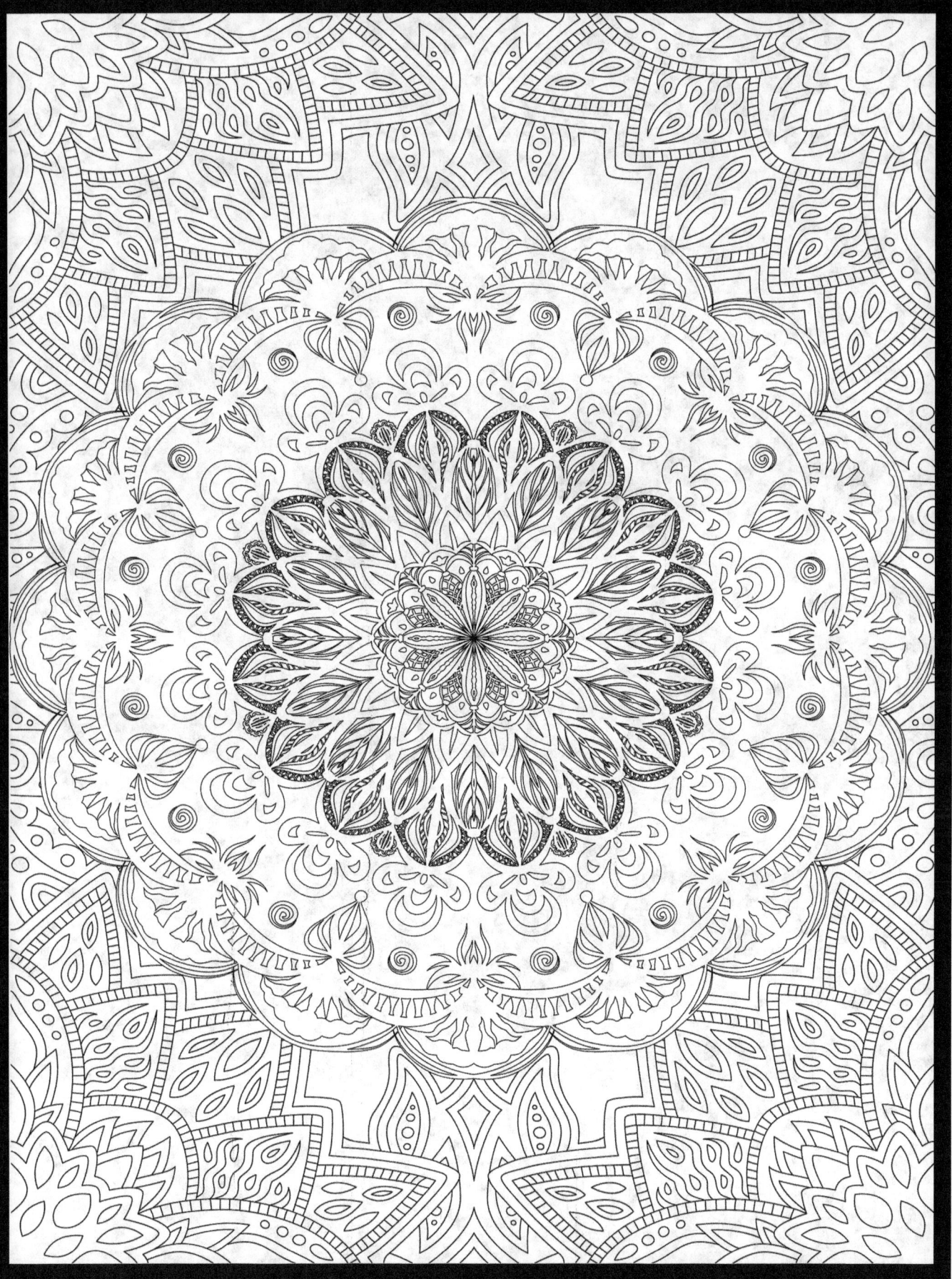

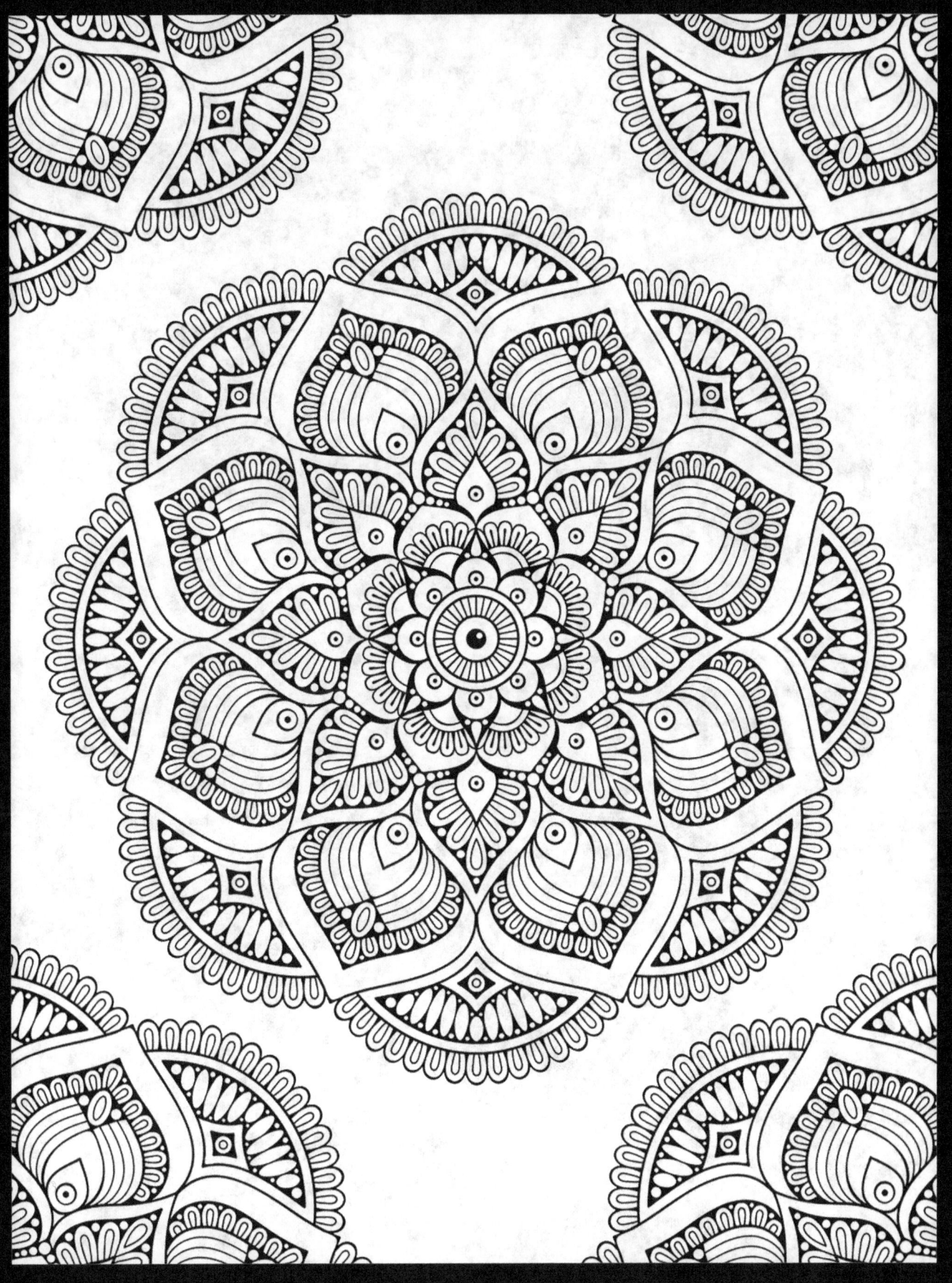

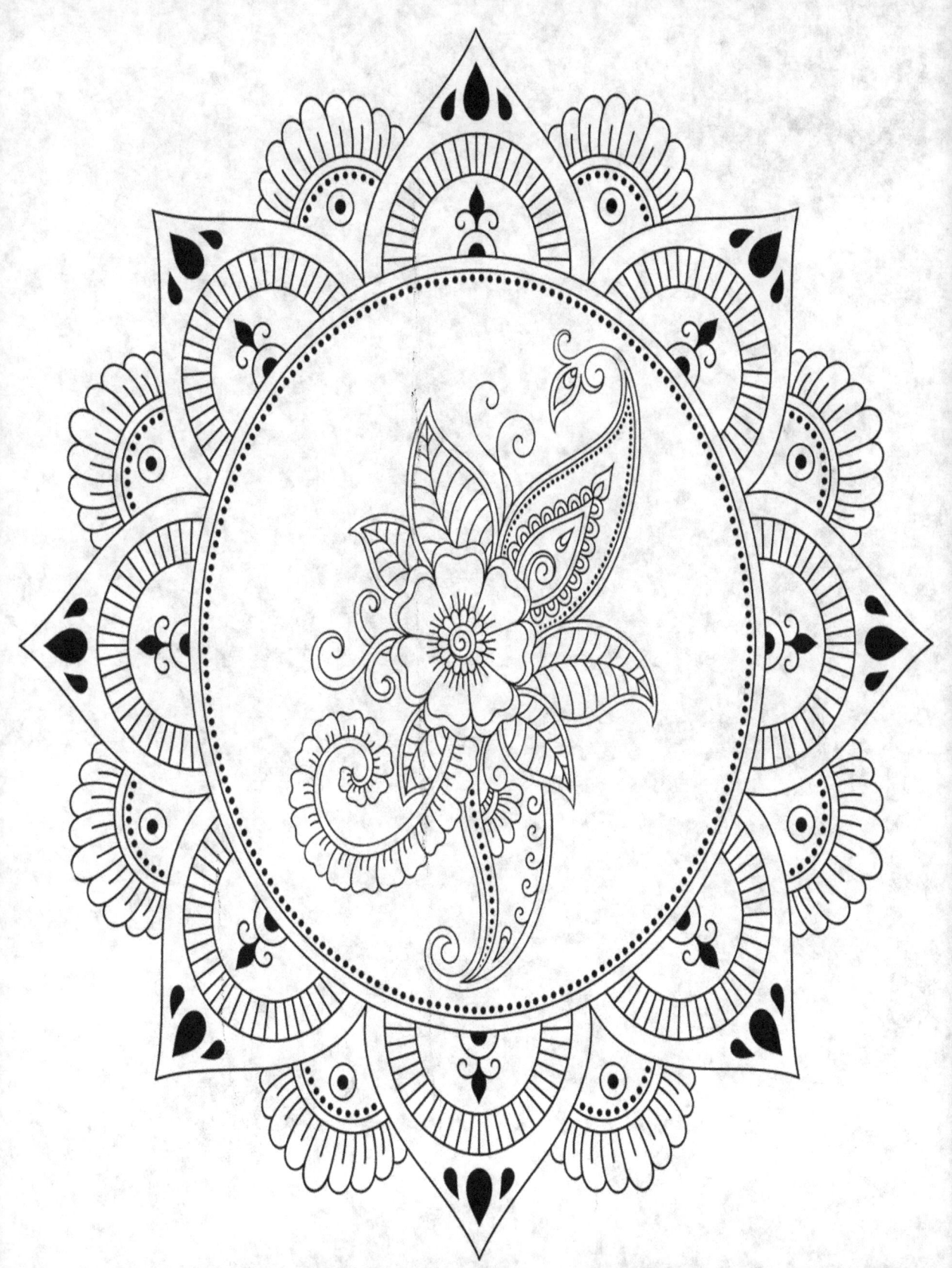

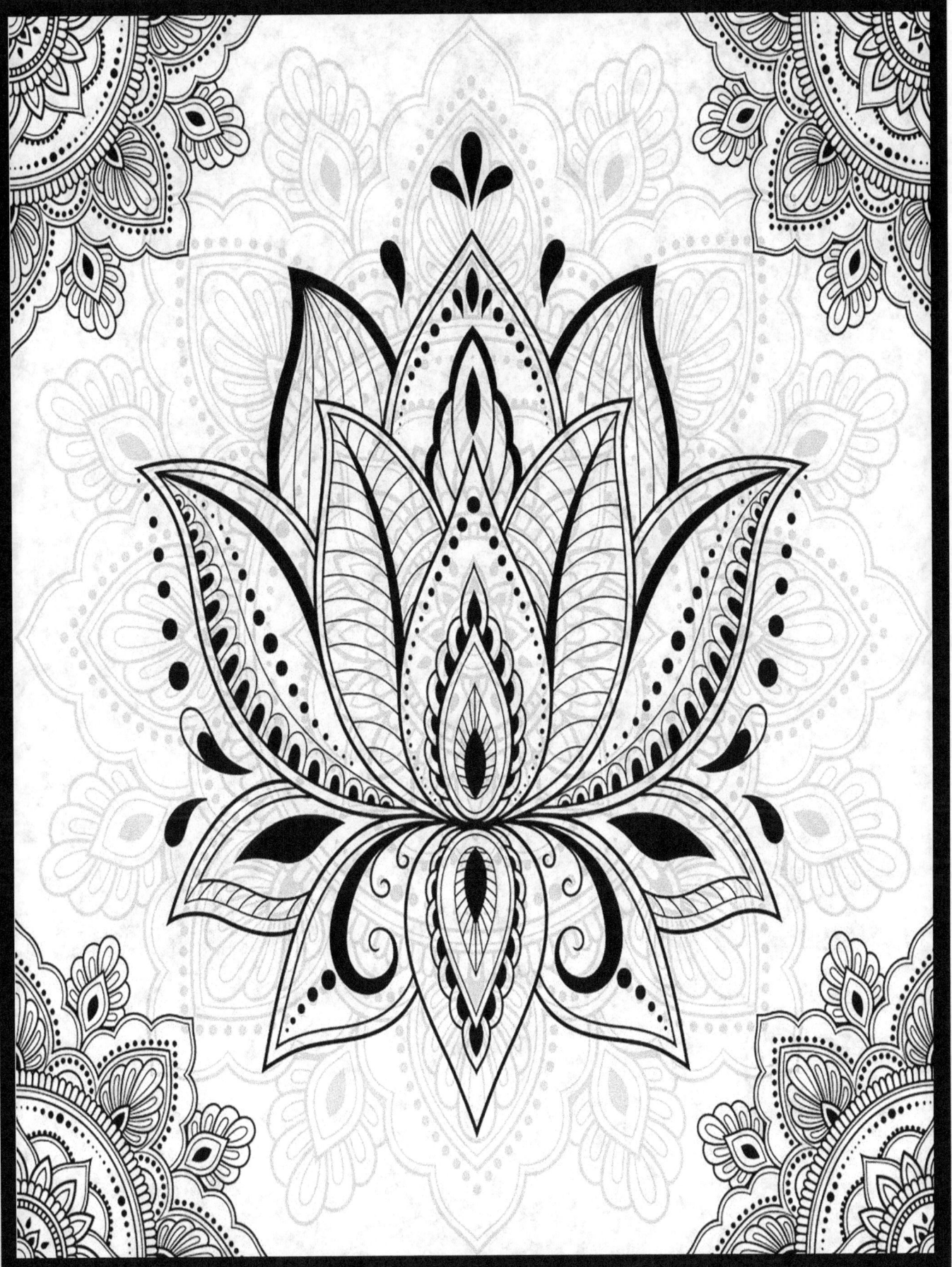

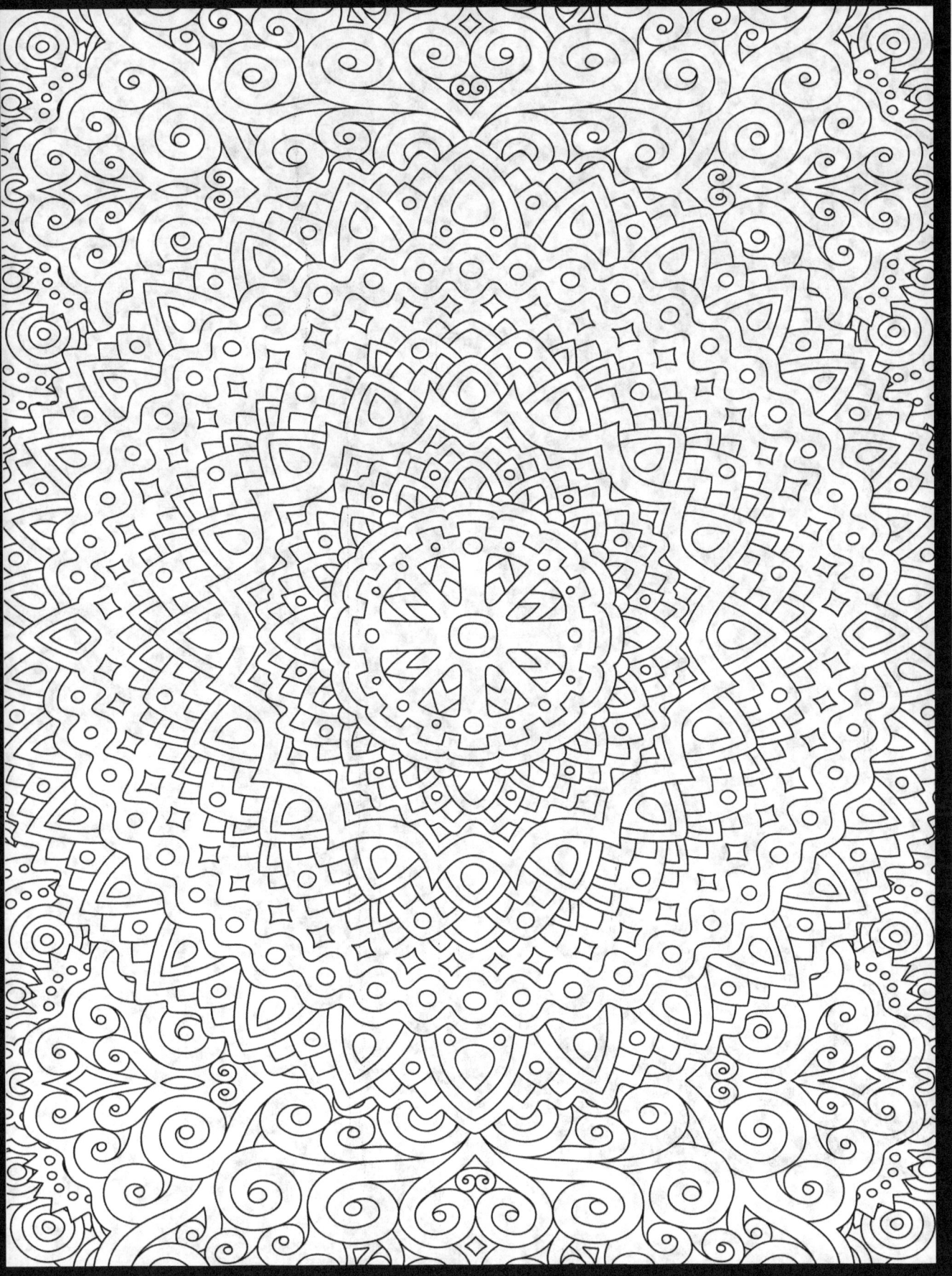

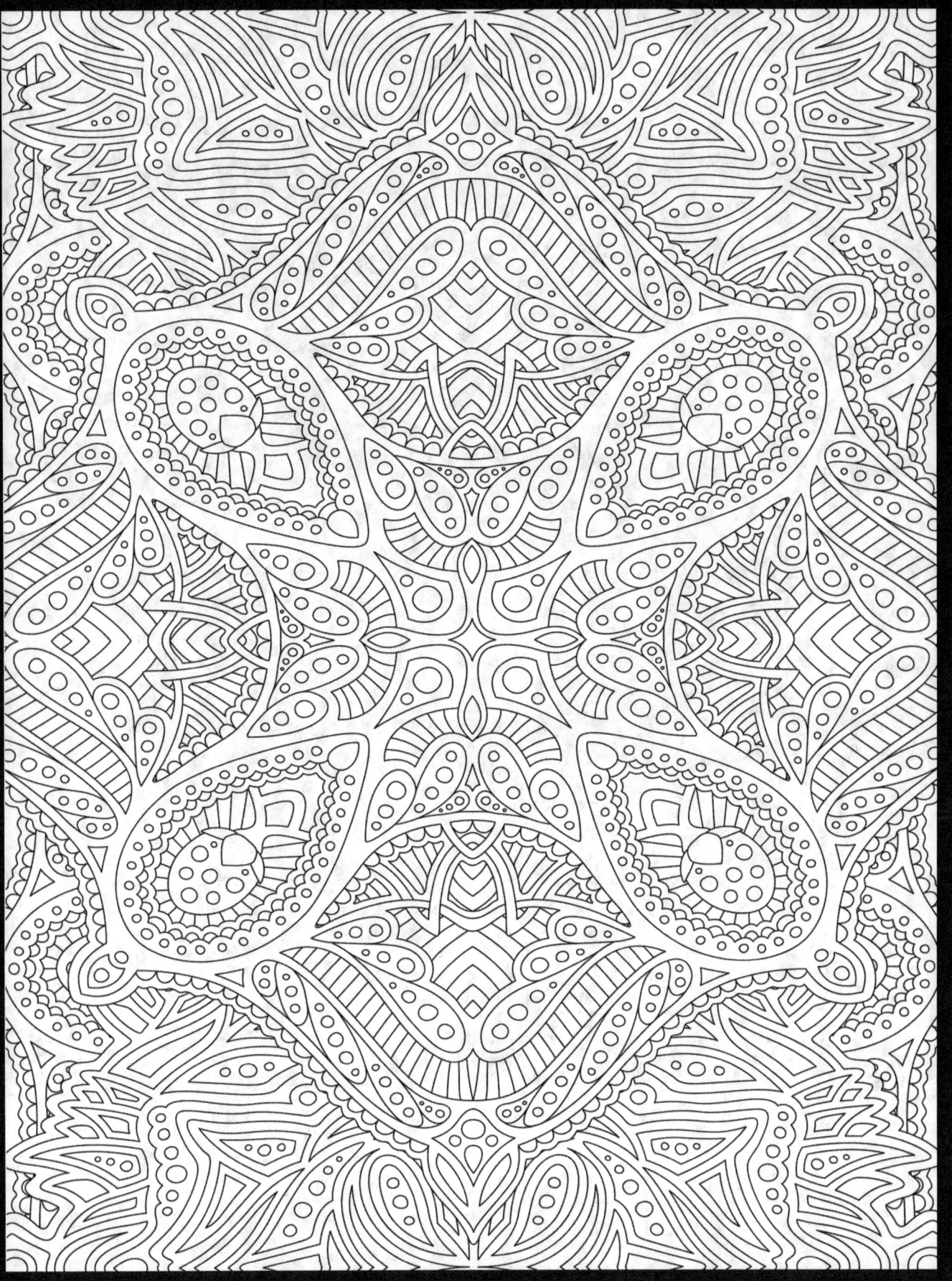

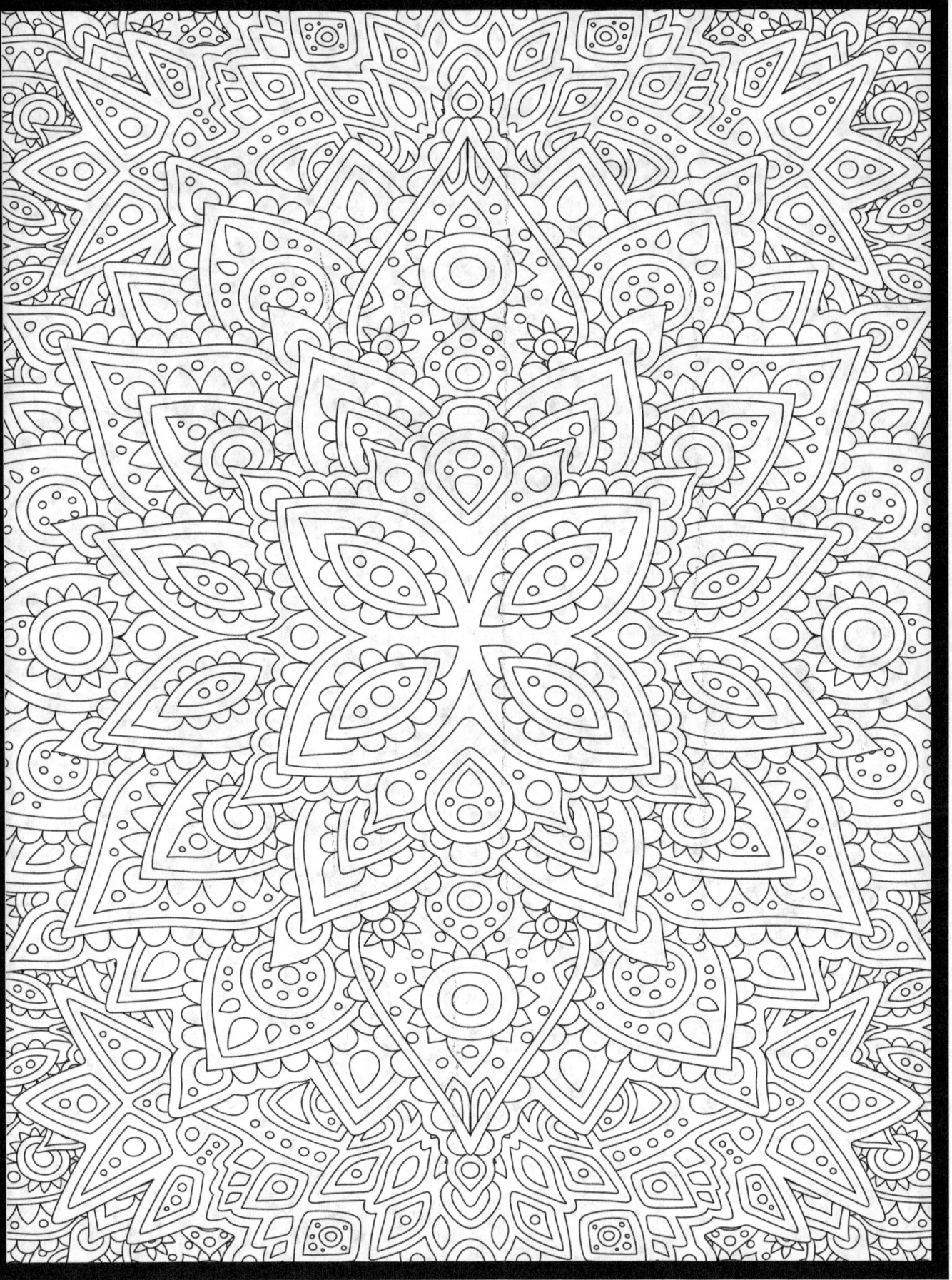

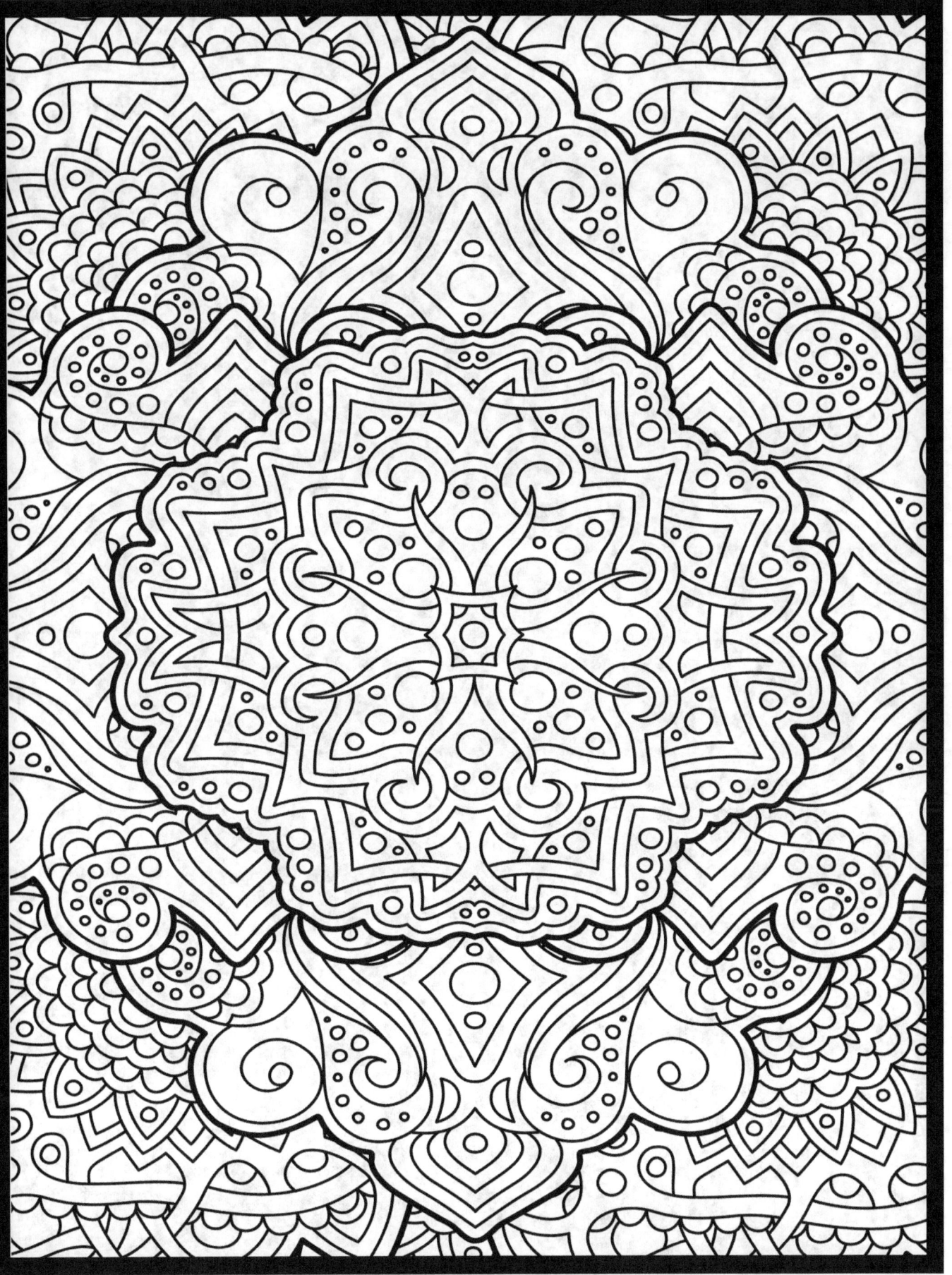

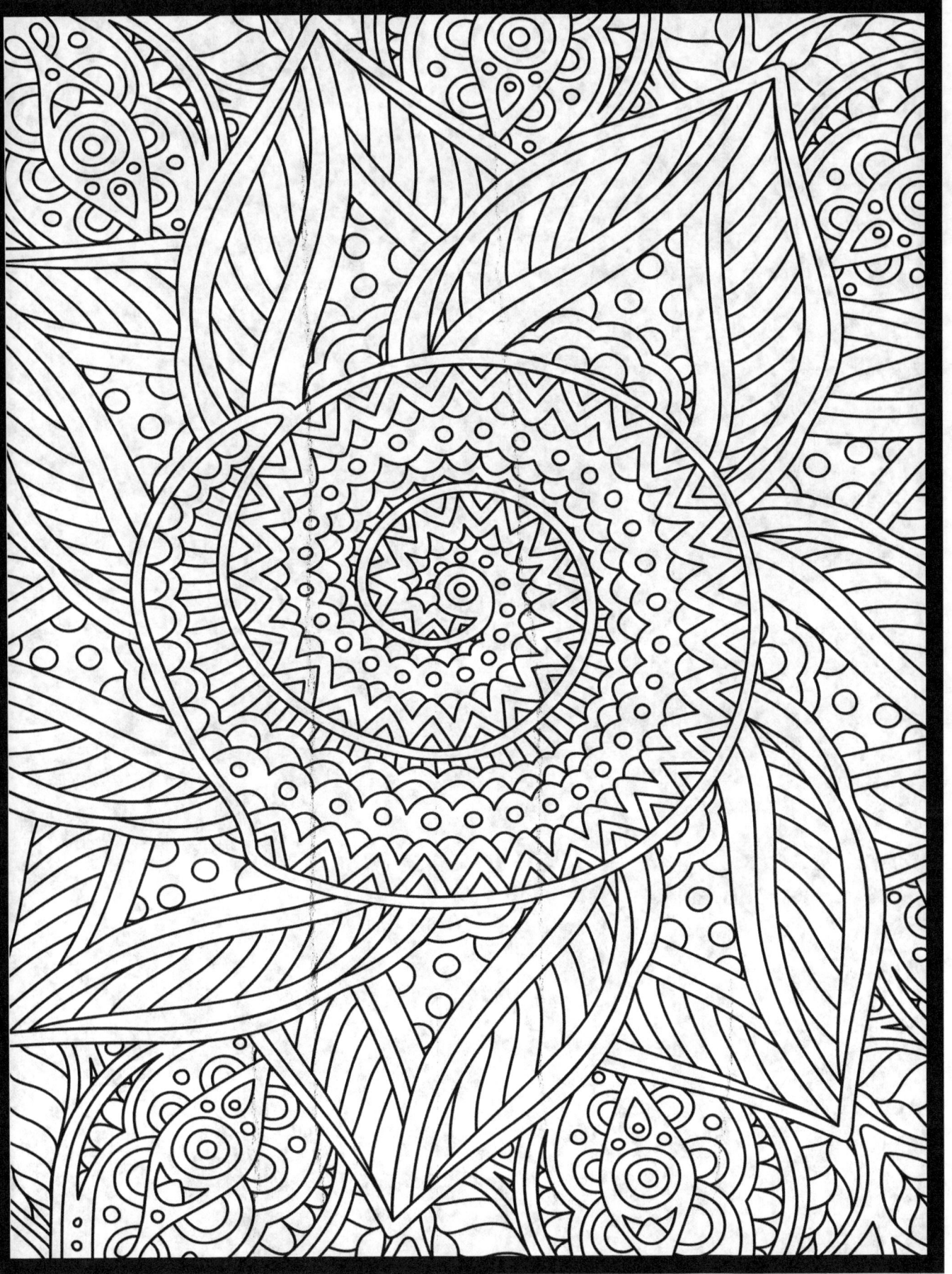

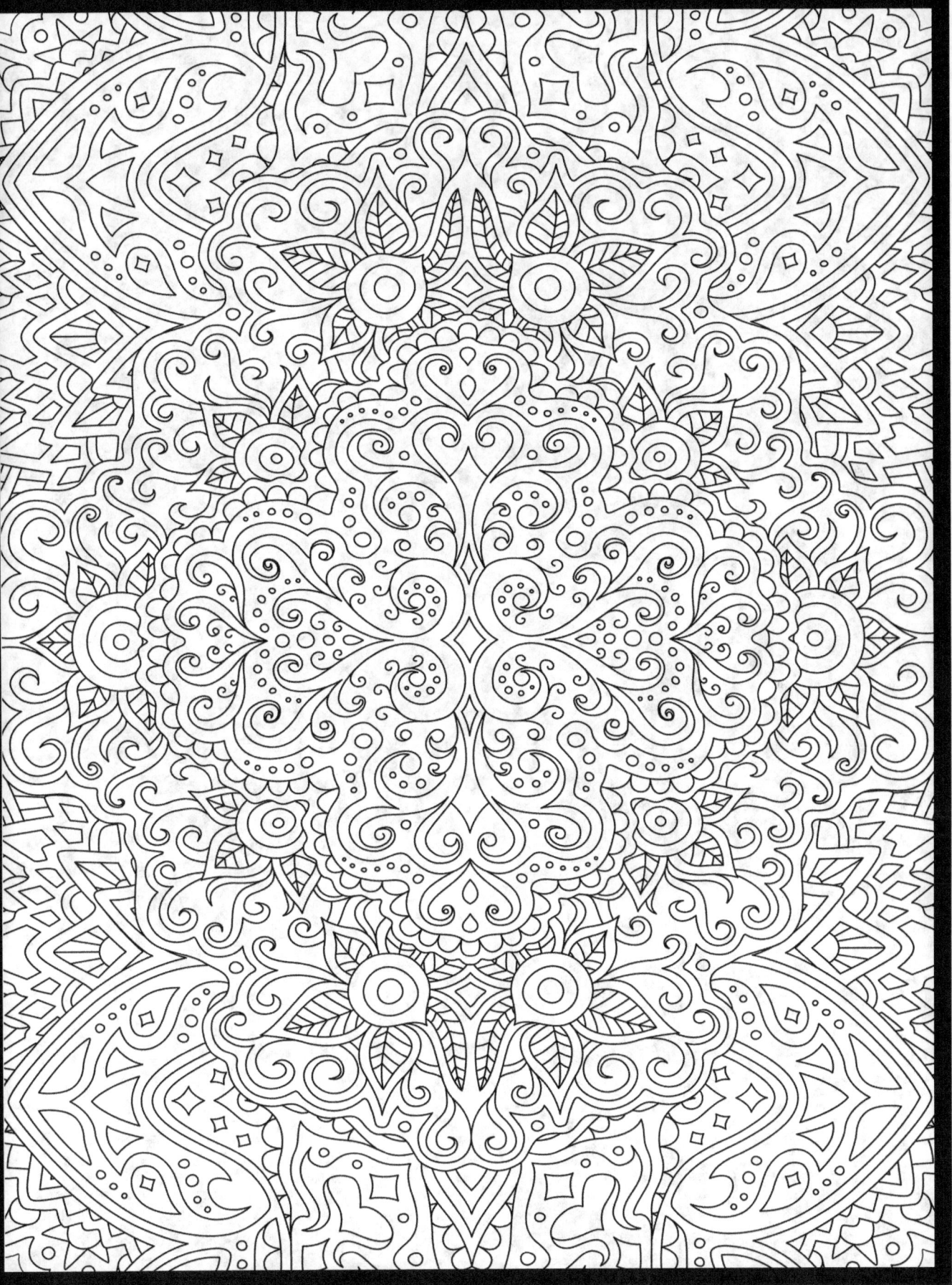

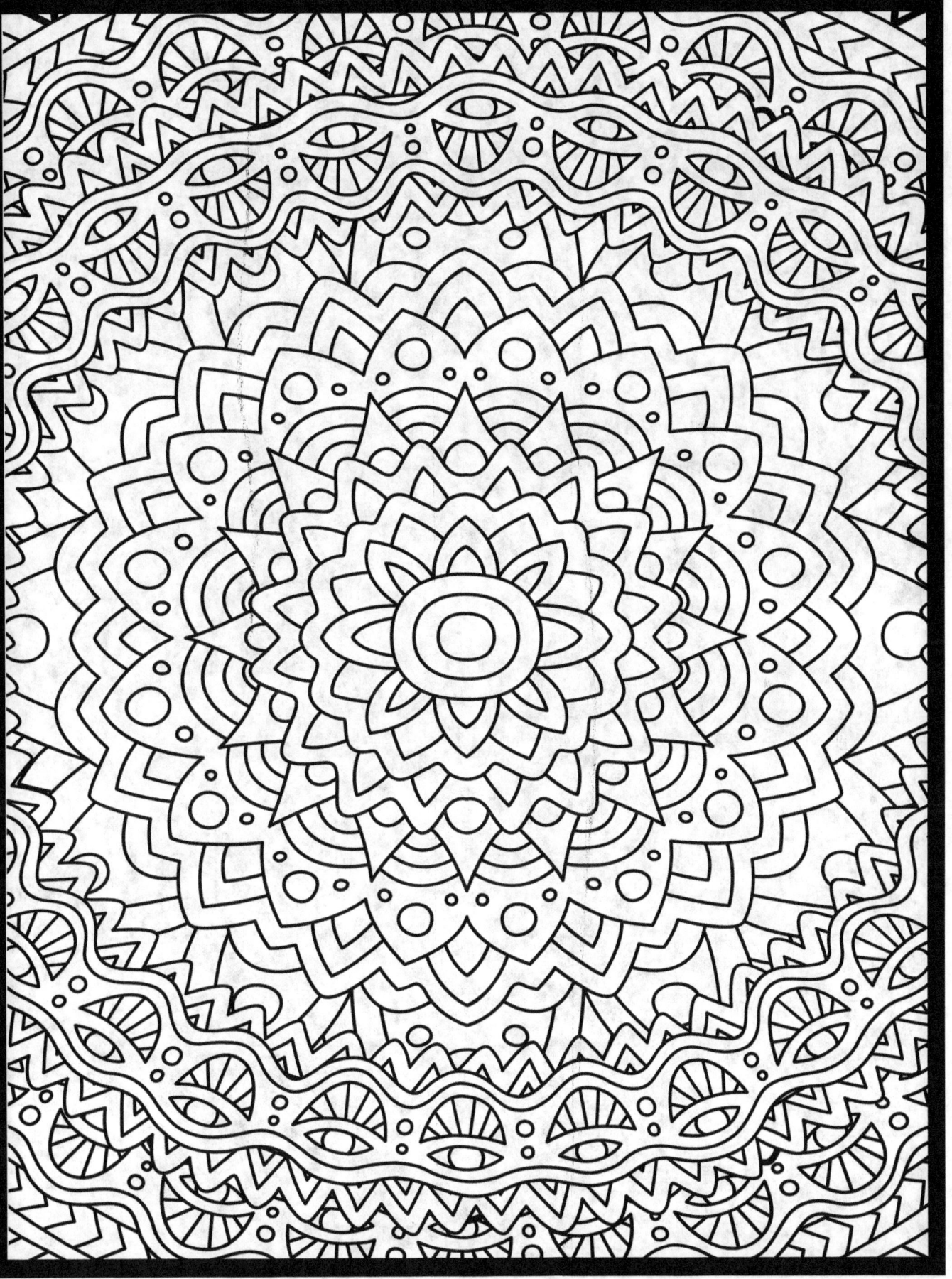

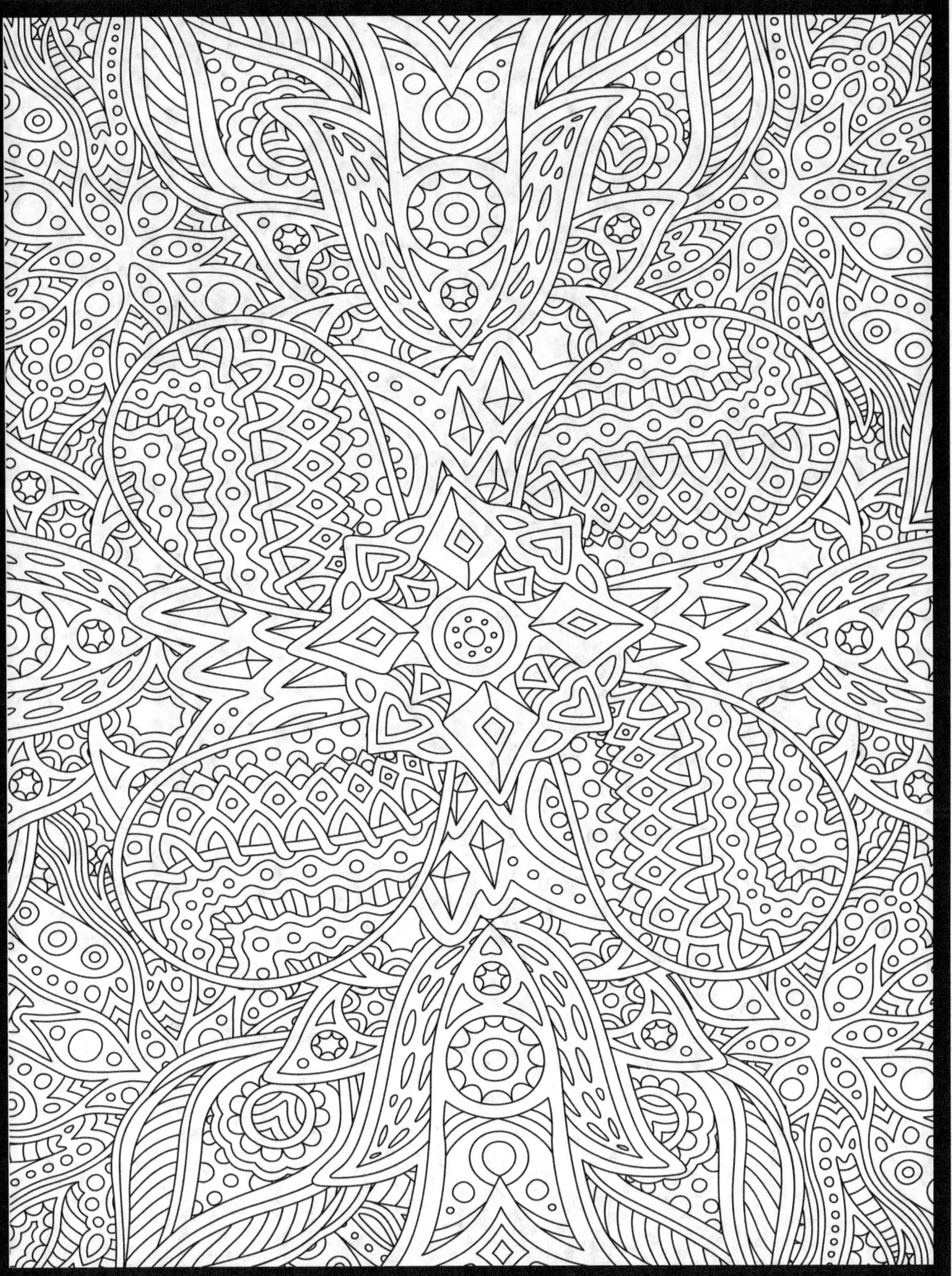

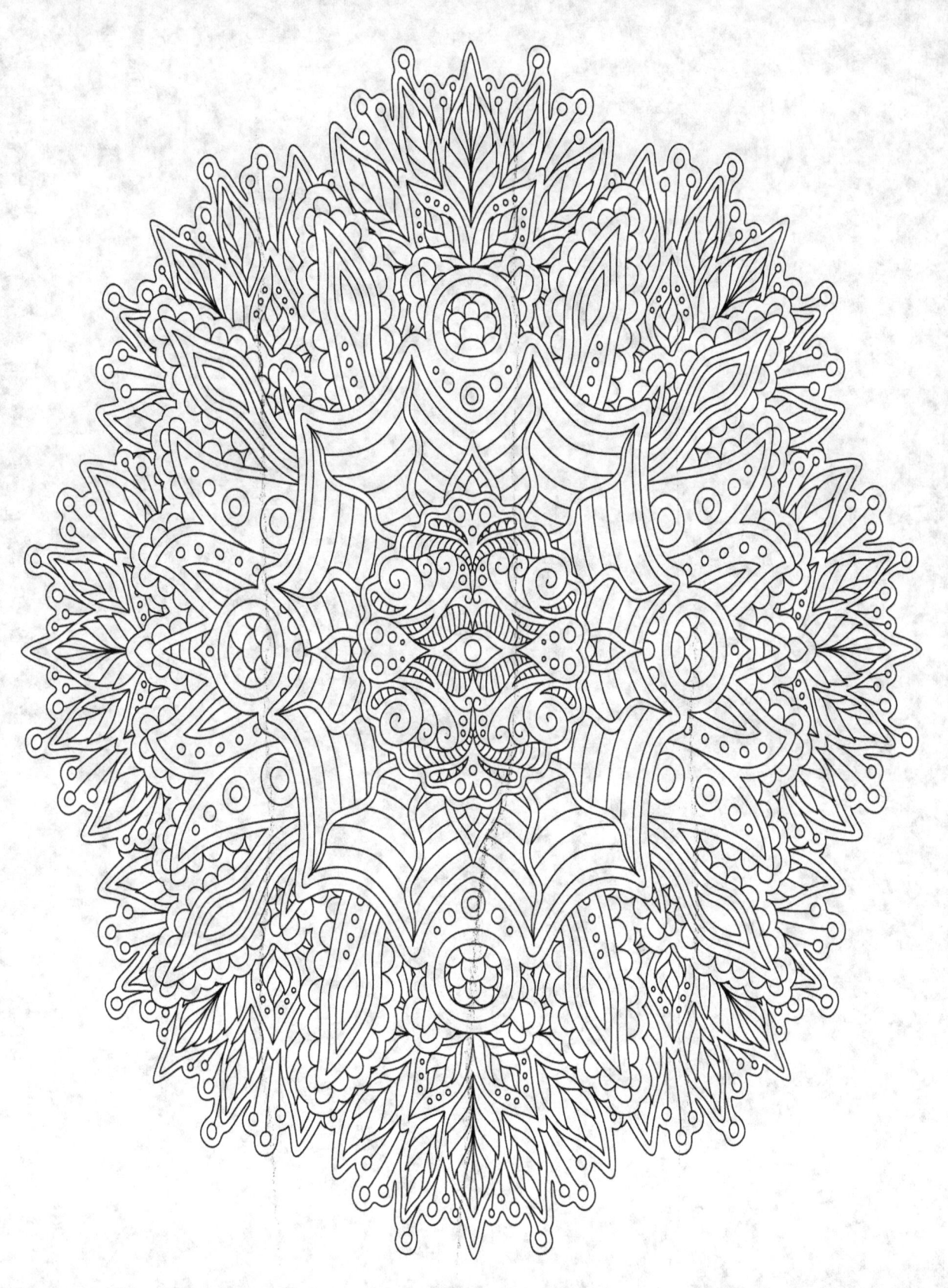

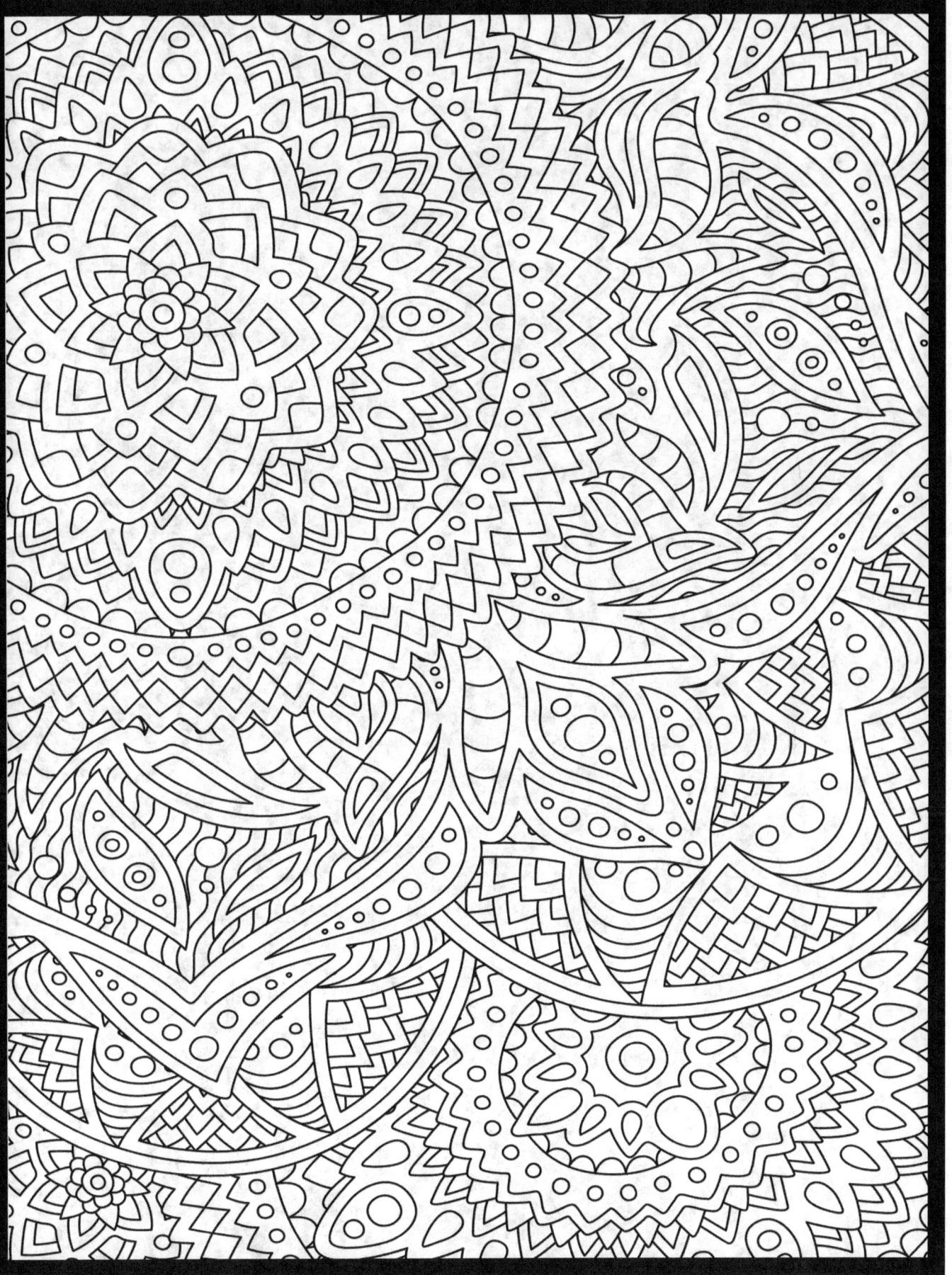

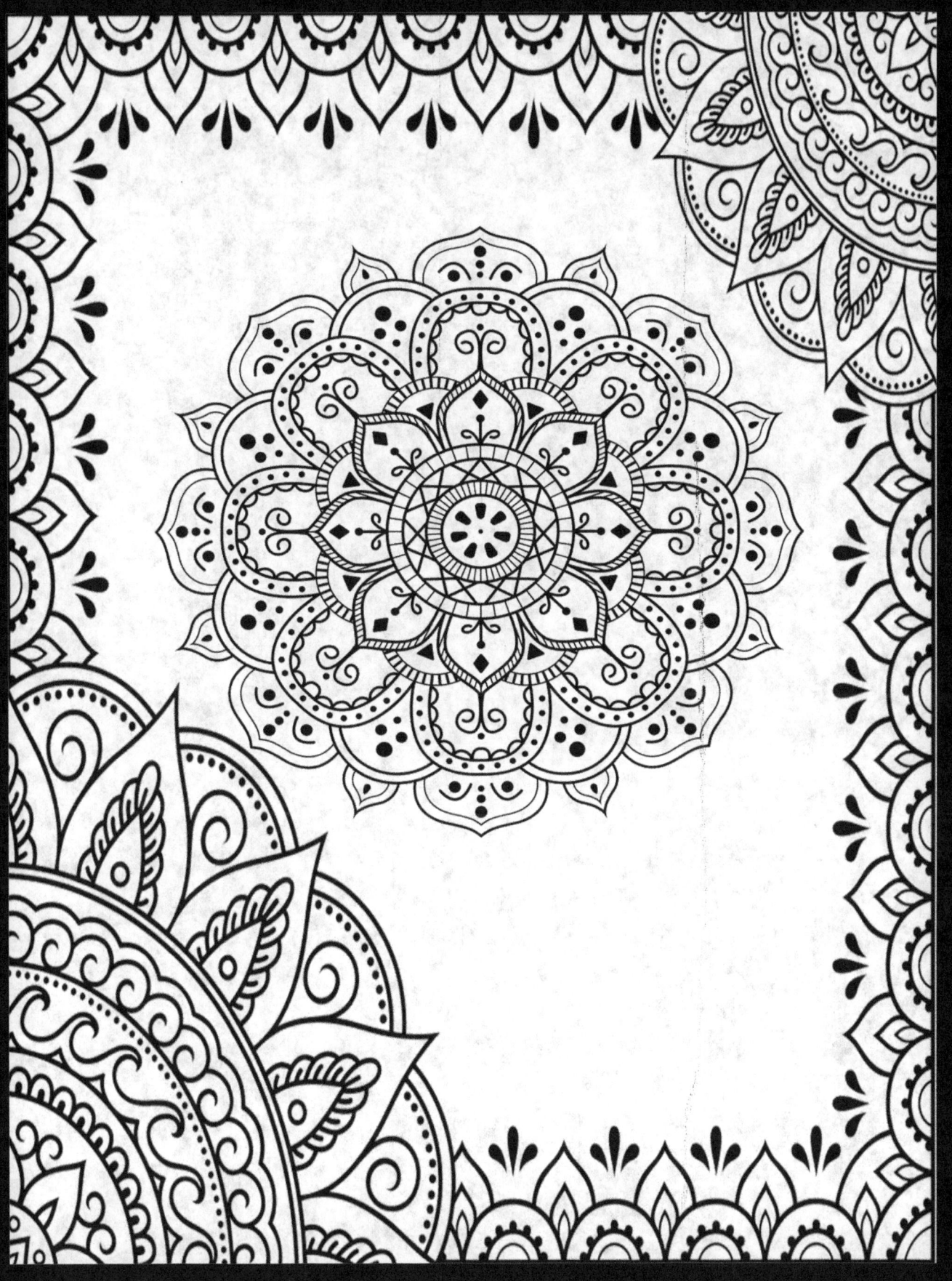

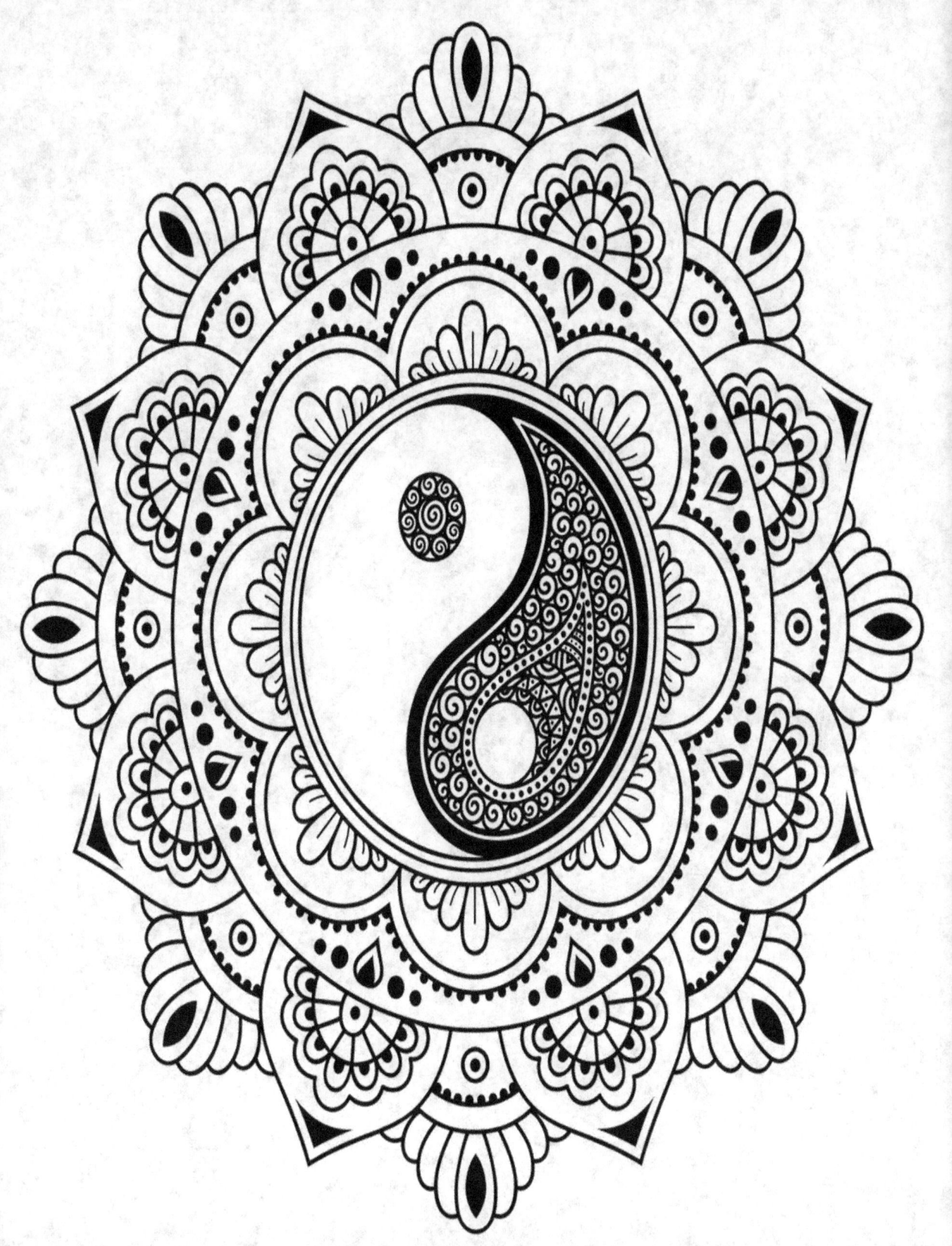

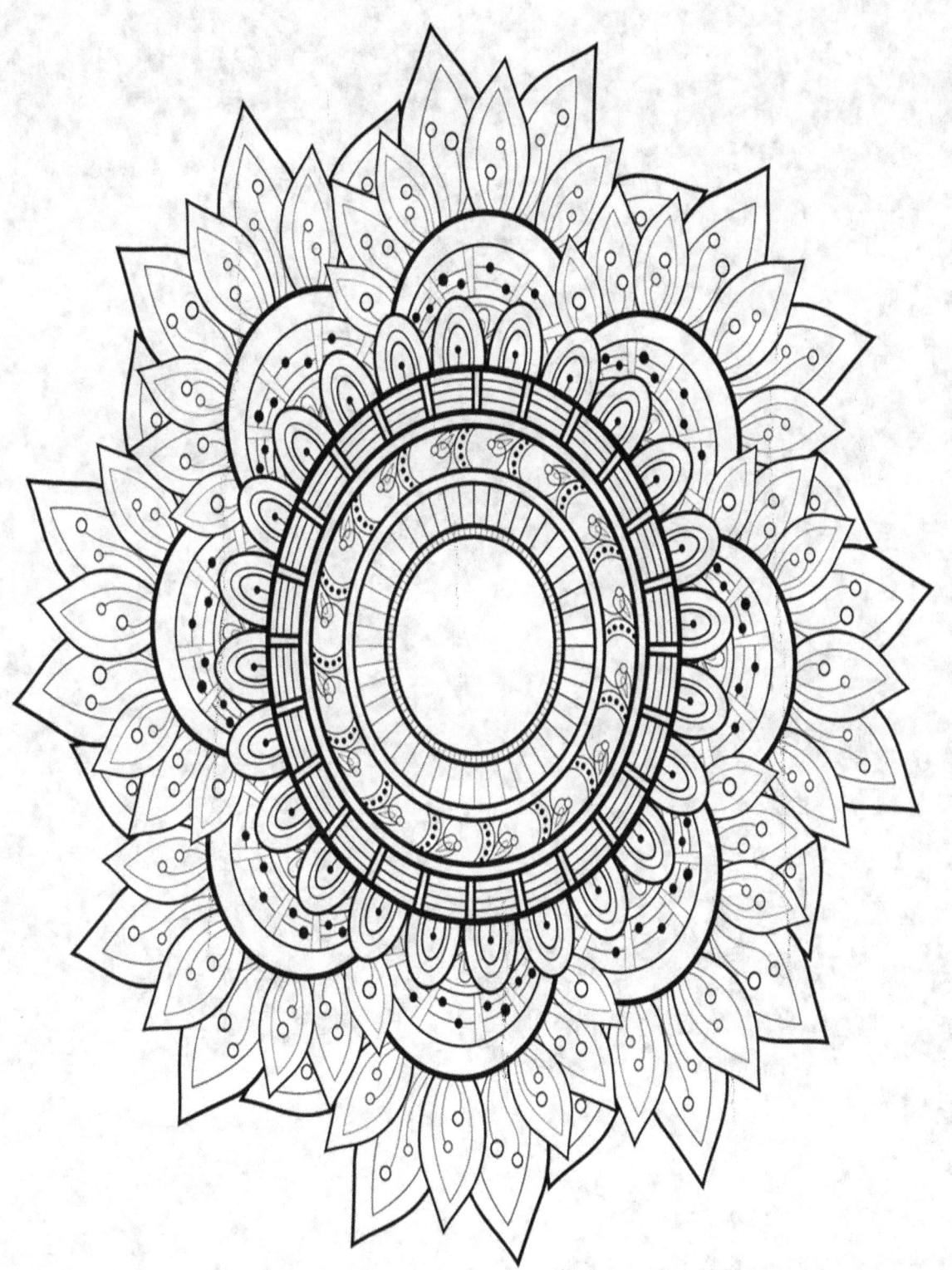

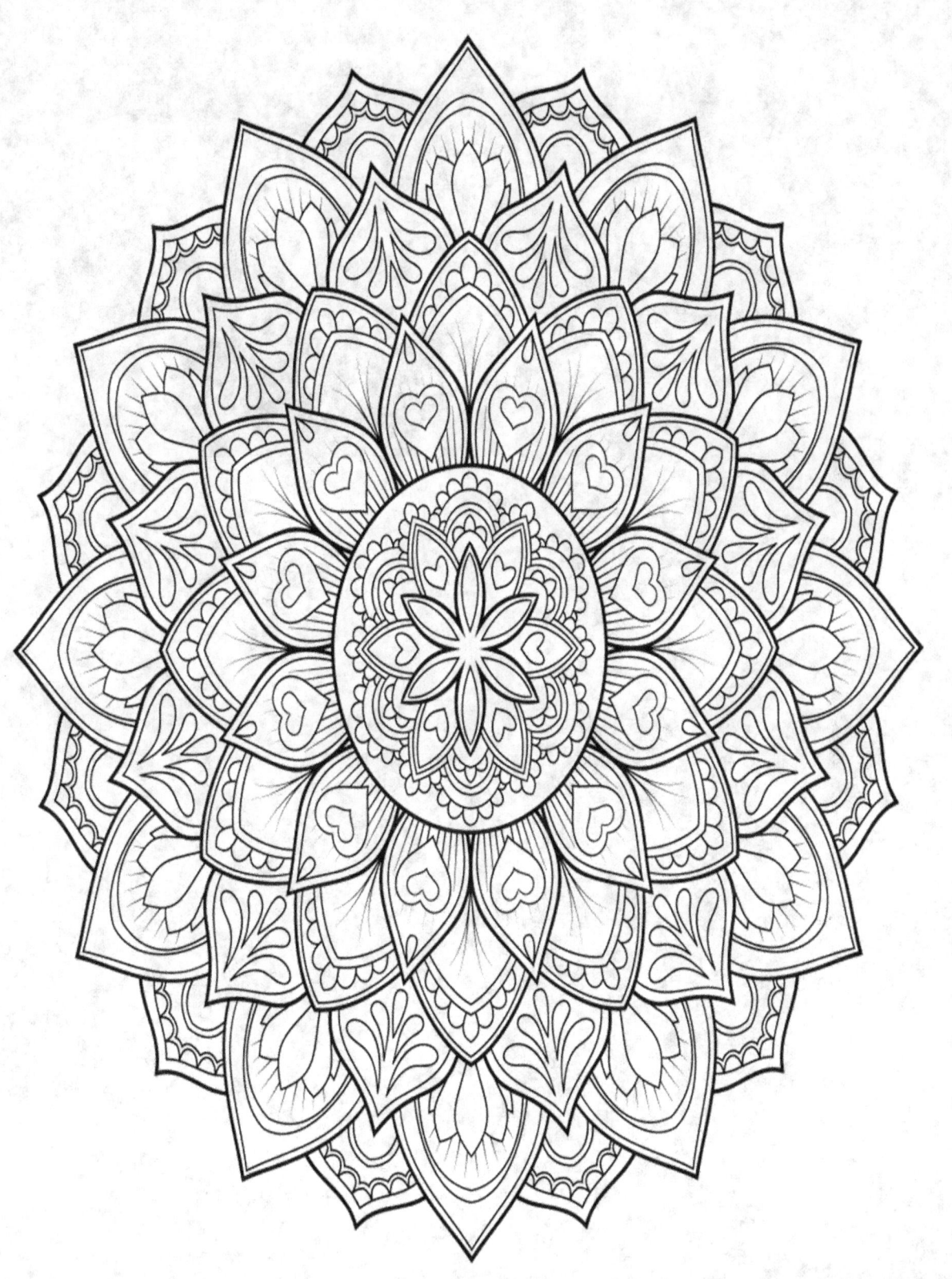

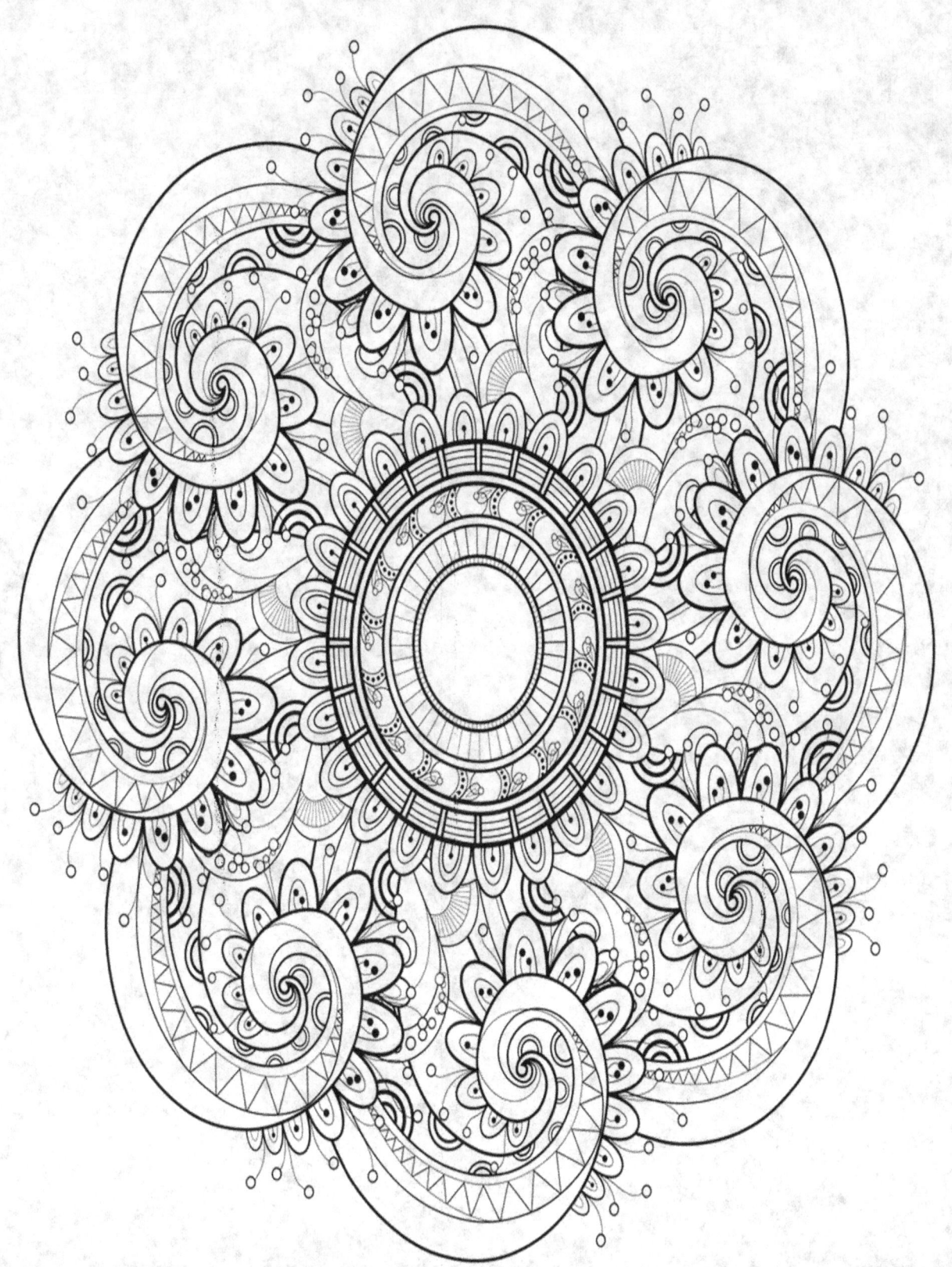

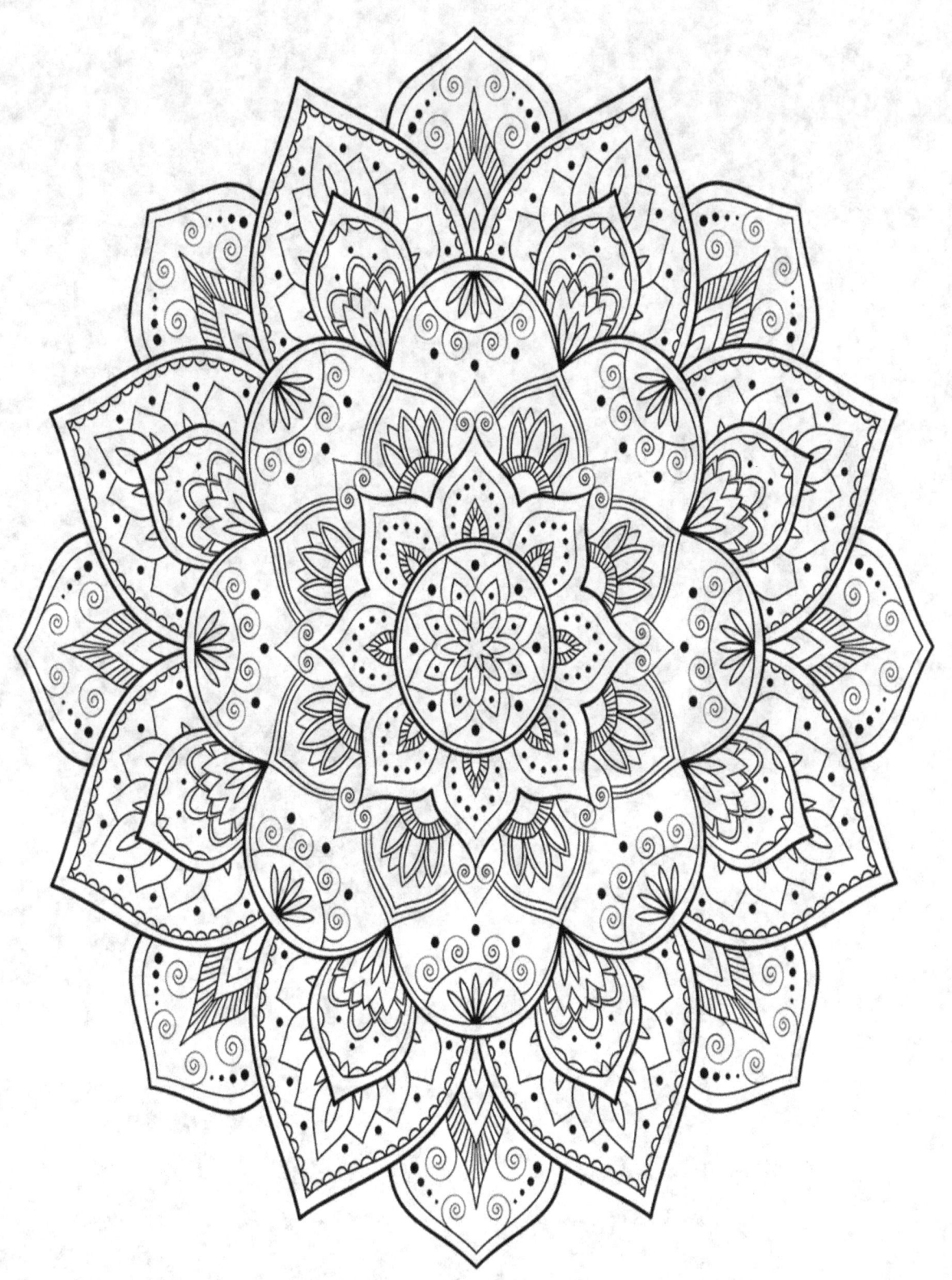

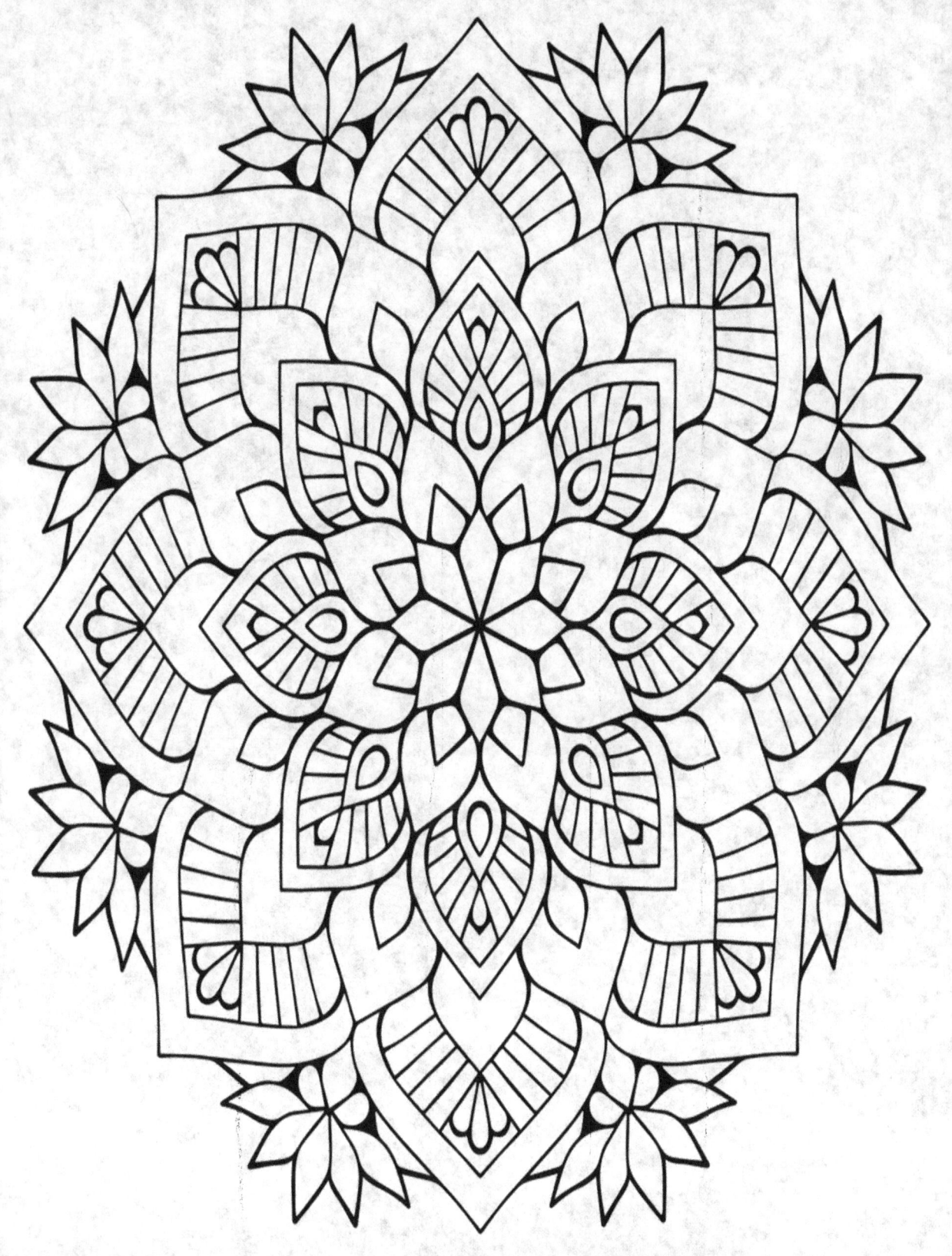

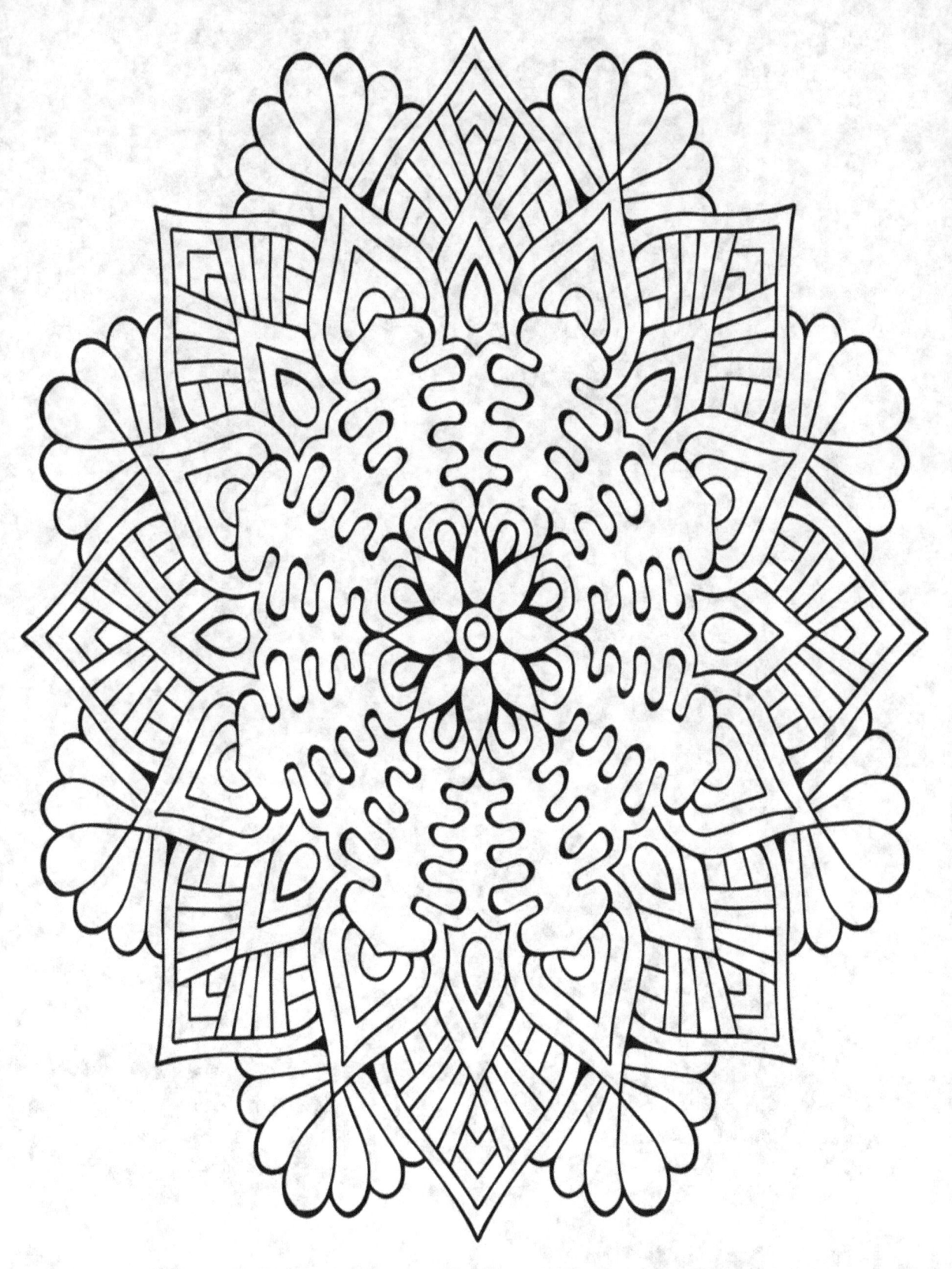

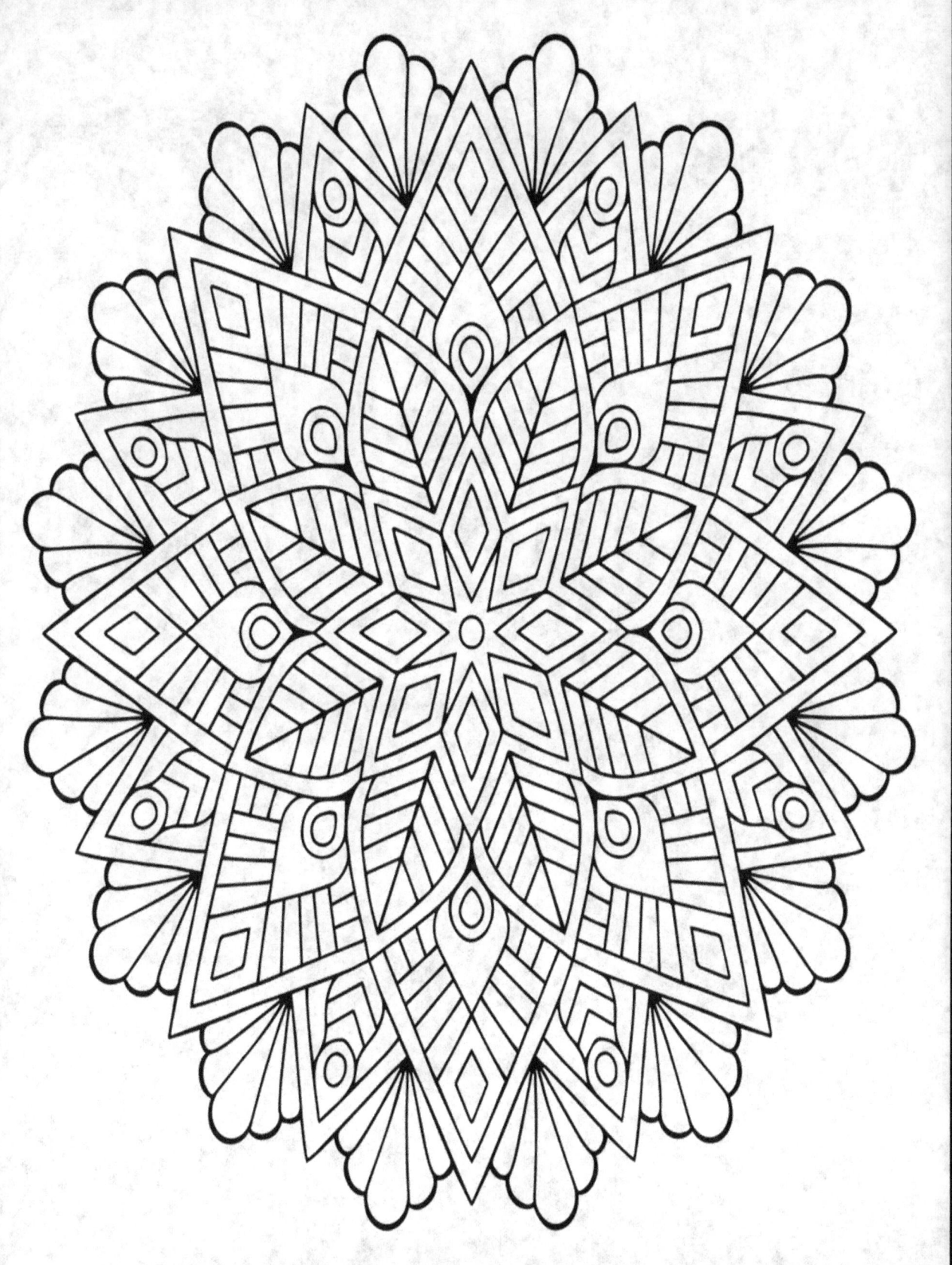

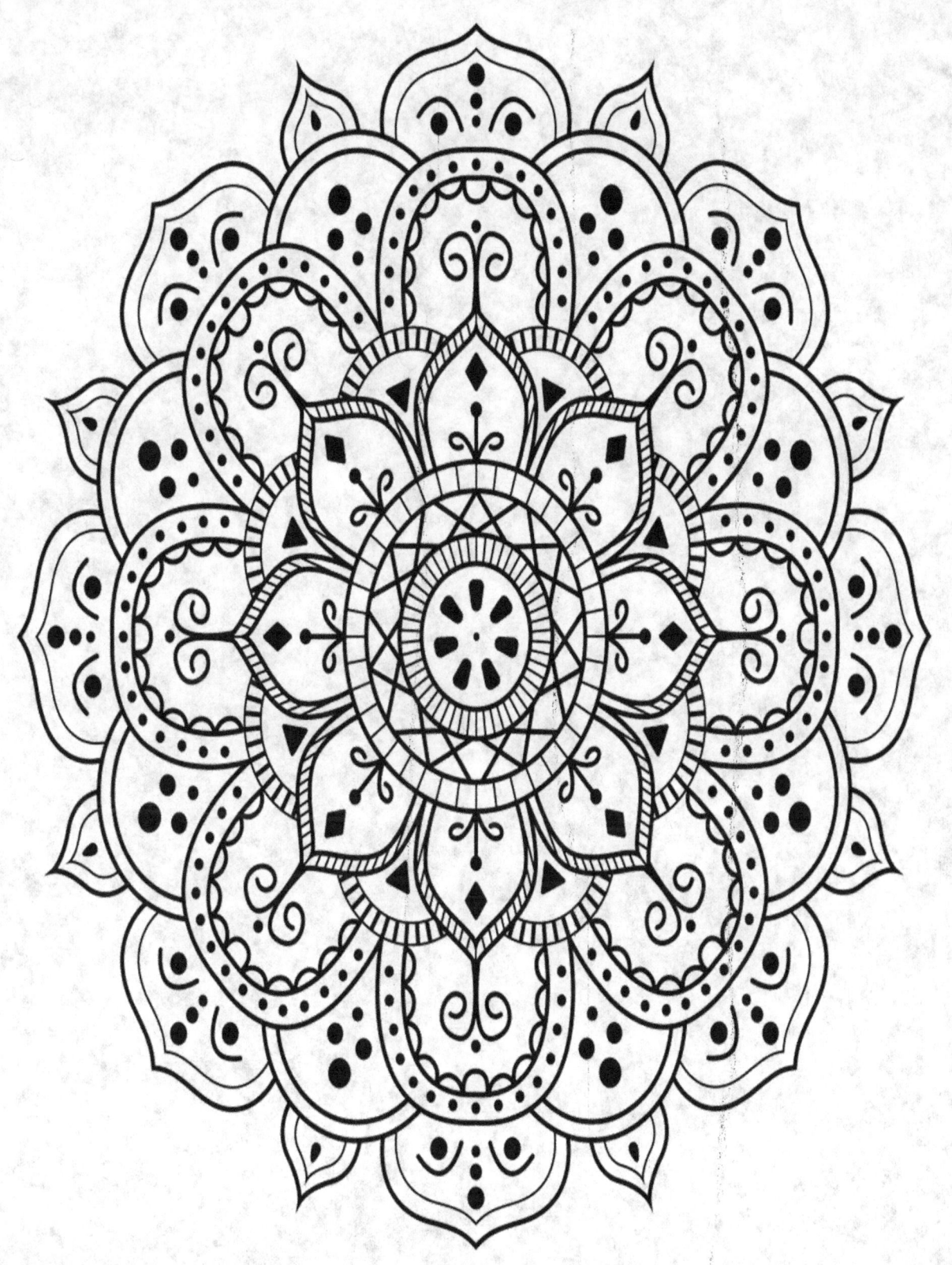

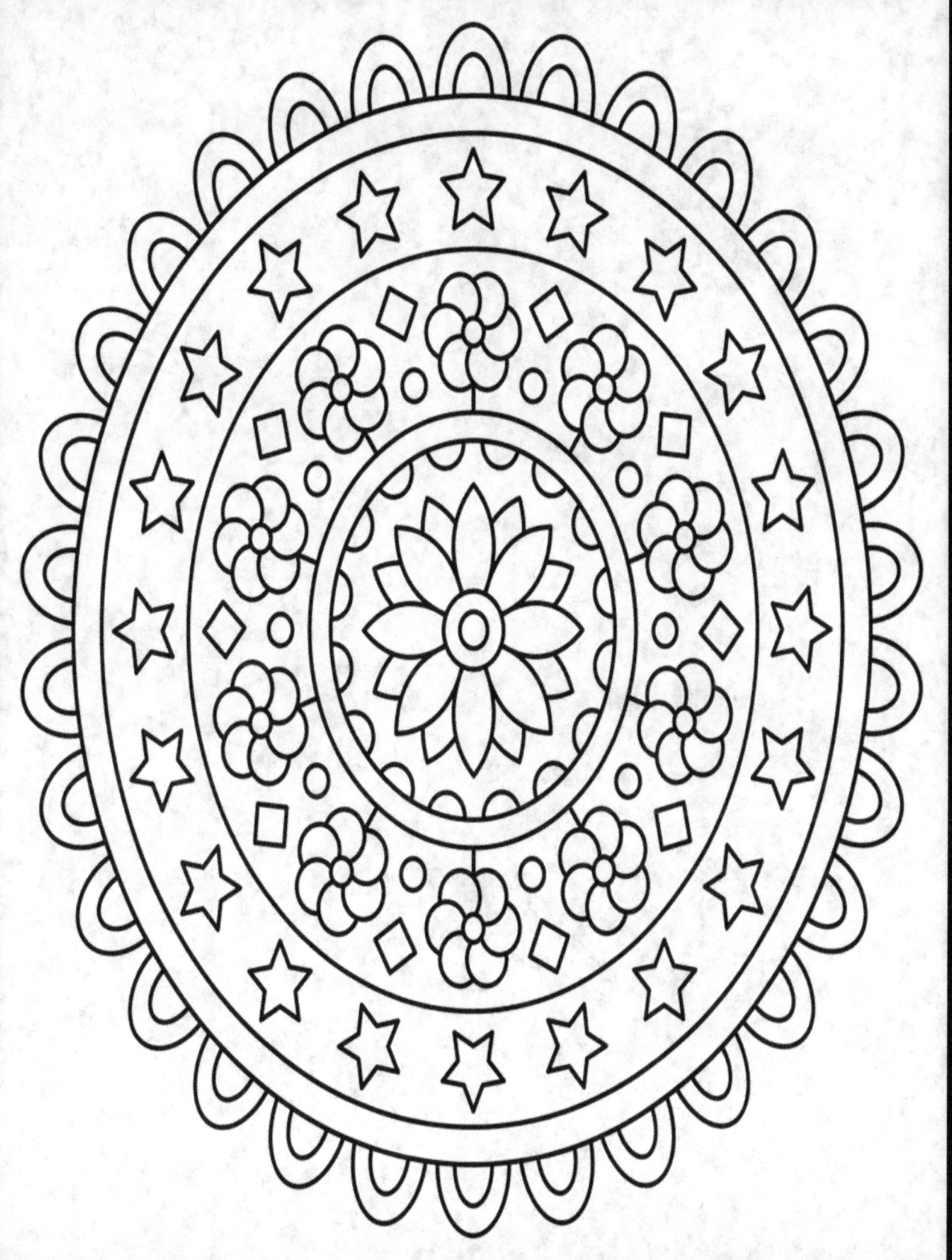

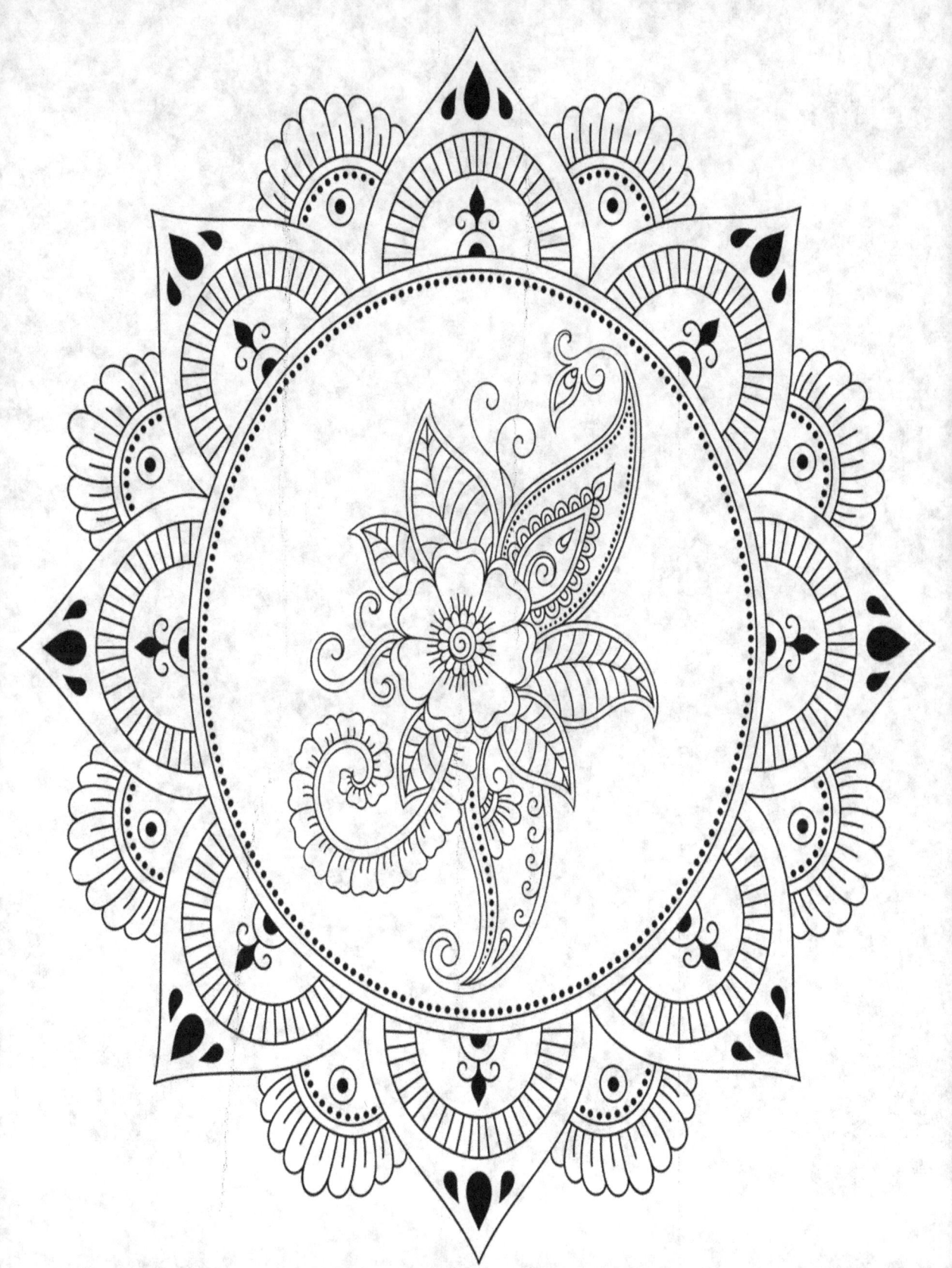

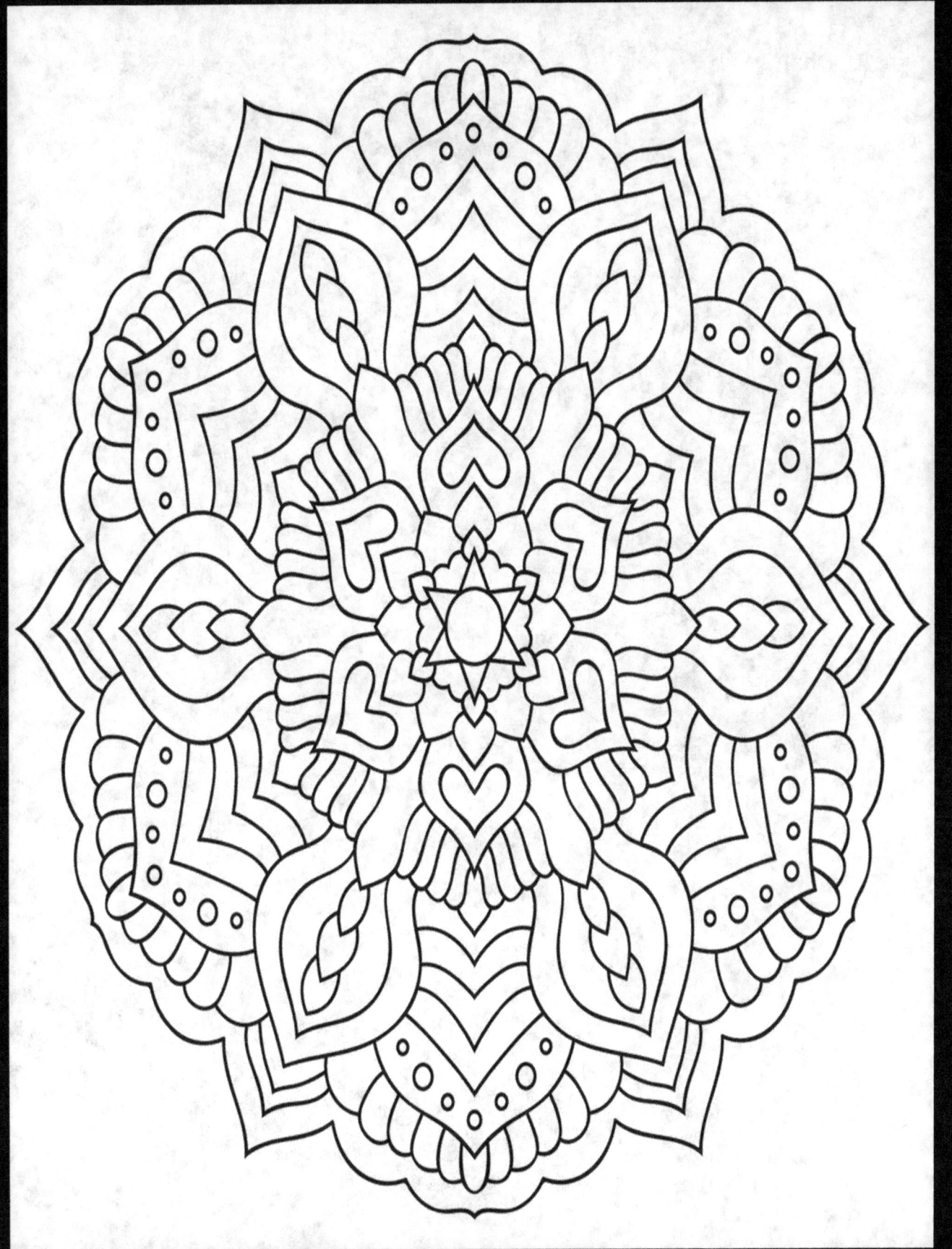

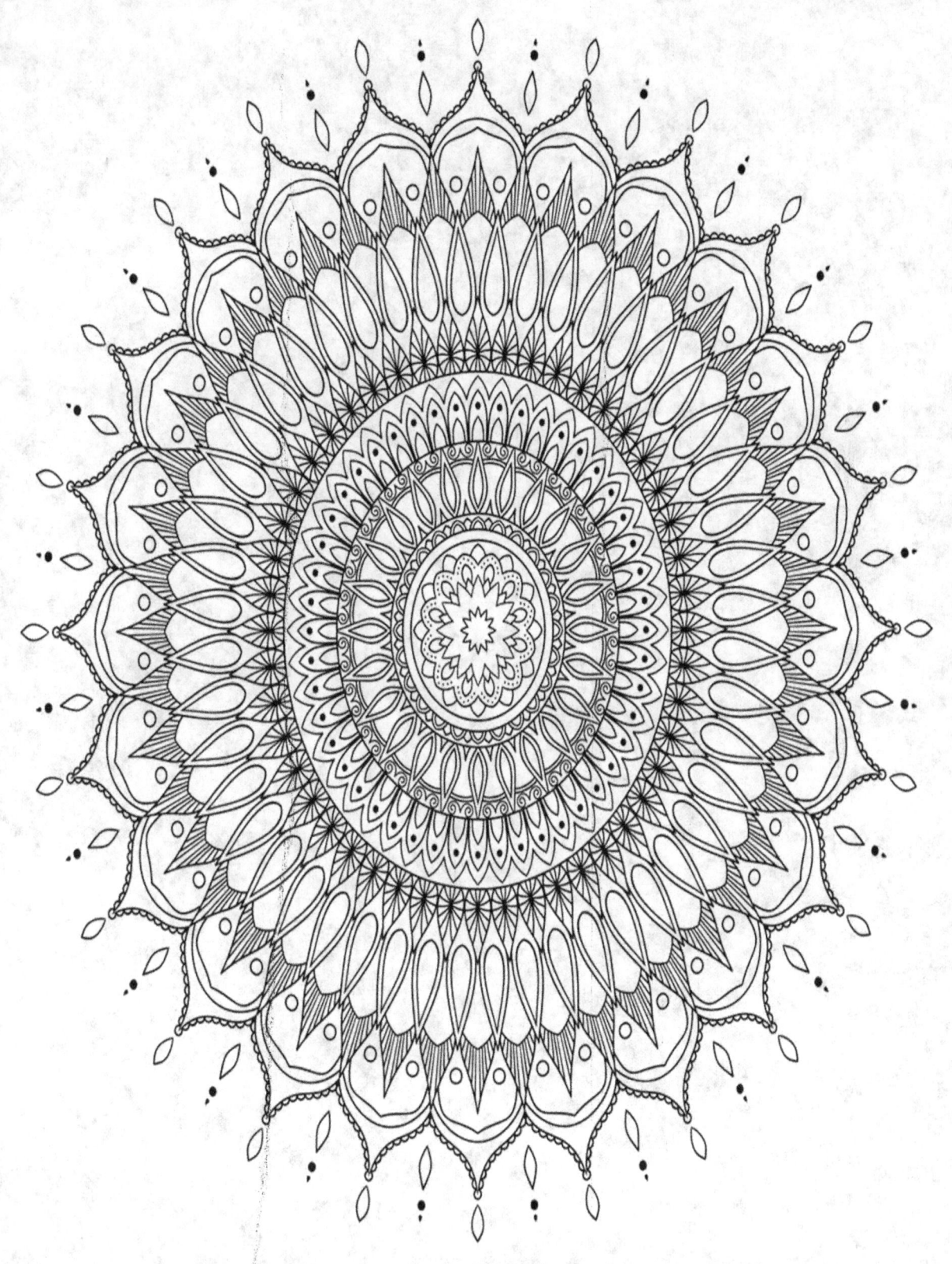

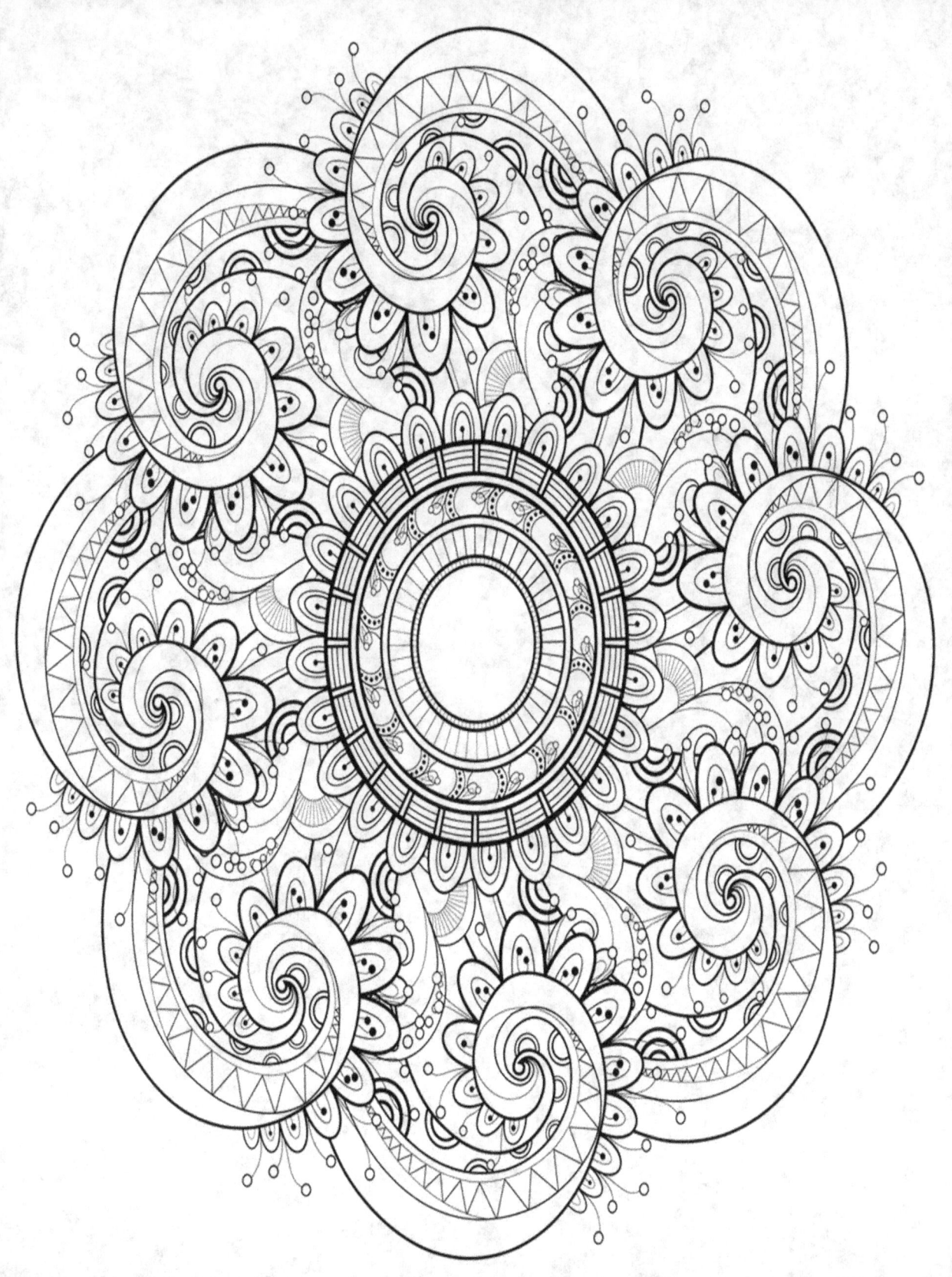

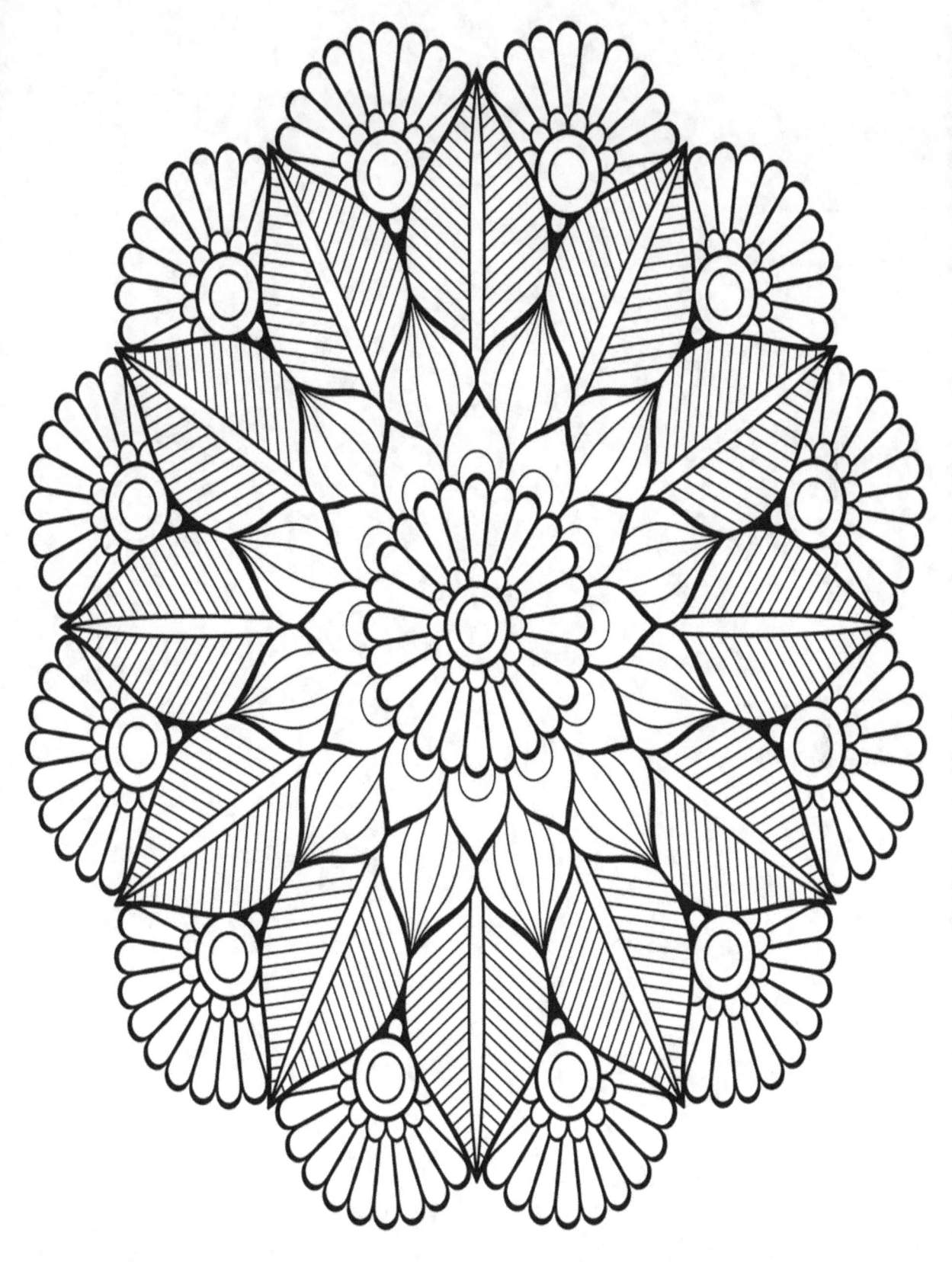

www.ingramcontent.com/pod-product-compliance
Lightning Source LLC
Chambersburg PA
CBHW080513220526
45465CB00006B/2474